GREAT YARMOUTH
AND THE
GREAT WAR

The Home Front

Colin Tooke

First Published 2014
by
Colin Tooke
8 Reginald Court
Estcourt Road
Great Yarmouth. NR30 4LJ

L940.3426

ISBN 978-9556013-5-4

Printed in England by Blackwell Print & Marketing
Charles Street, Great Yarmouth, Norfolk NR30 3LA

2

CONTENTS

ACKNOWLEDGEMENTS

.

I would like to thank the many people who have helped me with information and advice during the course of writing this book. This includes Peter Allard, for his researches into the Auxiliary Patrol Base and information about fishing vessels. Perry Watson for allowing me to use material and images from his researches. Jo O'Donoghue, curator at the Time & Tide Museum for giving me access to the archives held there. Charles Lewis, for allowing me to use material from his researches compiled in the 1980s. Graham Brown, volunteer at the Great Yarmouth Library, for his patience and help during my several visits there and to Peter Jones for allowing me to copy images from his postcard collection. Once again John Simmons has corrected my grammar and punctuation and as usual my wife Jan has shown great patience while I have been locked away producing this book.

A scale model of the Royal Naval Air Station,
(see page 62), was made in the 1970s by four local model makers, L. Elphick, T.Overill, D. Myhill and B. Scott. Originally displayed in the Maritime Museum, the model is now on display at the Flixton Aircraft Museum, Bungay. The pictures of the model are reproduced by courtesy of the Flixton Museum.

INTRODUCTION

Great Yarmouth can claim a unique, if little known, place in the history of the Great War. It was the first place in Great Britain to be attacked from the sea by a hostile enemy force when bombarded by German warships in November 1914 and it became the first place to be subjected to an aerial attack two months later when German Zeppelin airships bombed the town in January, 1915. Two of the town's residents unfortunately became the first people in the country to die as a result of an aerial attack.

Aeroplanes from the town's Air Station were among the pioneers in developing techniques to destroy German airships and many drifters and trawlers from the local fishing fleet, with their local crews, played an important role in submarine deterrent warfare. Great Yarmouth was, as it would be in the next world conflict, a Front Line Town of strategic importance.

When Britain declared war on Germany on 4 August 1914 new warfare technology was developing rapidly and this was to make the Great War different to any other major conflict in history. On land, men on horseback would no longer be the dominant fighting force: after a few months of trench warfare the tank was designed to destroy barbed wire defences and trenches and cross any no-man's land. In the air the airship and the aeroplane took war to places hitherto unreachable, while at sea newly-developed submarines would bring a different element to traditional sea battles.

The fear of invasion ran high along the East Coast and plans were made to evacuate the town if the enemy landed. Great Yarmouth's position made it vulnerable to attack from the sea and, for the first time in history, from the air. Hundreds of troops were billeted in the town and coastal defences were hurriedly put in place. The town became an important naval base, submarine base and air station.

As the land war on the Western Front developed, the attitude that the war would be over by Christmas quickly changed. It was realised that this would not be a short conflict and indeed the war was to drag on for four long years, costing nine million soldiers their lives.

The Defence of the Realm Act was passed on 8 August 1914, allowing the government to increase its control over people's lives. It suddenly became unlawful to fly kites, light bonfires, buy binoculars or discuss military matters. Beer was watered down and public houses had restricted opening hours. British Summer Time, a scheme to extend daylight-working time and save energy, identity cards. conscription, blackout and ration books were introduced. Many of these schemes would re-appear some thirty years later as the country faced another world conflict.

For the first time in history large numbers of women joined the workforce. The town's economy was to become devastated by the war, loss of income from both the fishing industry and the holiday trade brought great hardship to both the population and the Corporation, who at one point in the war were ready to declare themselves bankrupt. Three days after the war began the Treasury issued one pound and ten shilling (50p) notes in an effort to remove gold sovereigns from circulation to try and protect the country's gold reserves.

Over 7,000 men from the town either volunteered or were conscripted into the forces to fight for their country in the Great War. Of these, 1,472 lost their lives on active service, their names recorded on the memorial in St George's Park.

The battles on the Western Front and other overseas theatres of war have been documented in great detail over the years in many books. This book is about the Home Front, and how the war affected the town of Great Yarmouth and its people. More information about the military aspects of Great Yarmouth in the Great War could be researched in the National Archives at Kew, hopefully this book will lead other historians to further, more detailed, research.

Colin Tooke
2014.

THE PRE-WAR YEARS

Throughout the first decade of the twentieth century, Britain was becoming increasingly concerned at the developing political situation in Europe. The Napoleonic wars, a hundred years earlier, had put the south and east coast into a state of defence and now it appeared history was repeating itself: the Norfolk coast once again vulnerable to invasion.

Troops had been stationed in the town since the seventeenth century and, by the turn of the twentieth century, the relatively small Regular Army relied on Militia and Volunteer Forces, ready to be mobilised at any time of danger or invasion. In 1901 a small group of Yarmouth men from both the Militia and the Volunteers had returned from South Africa after volunteering to fight in the Boer War, the first time in the twentieth century men from the town had fought on foreign soil. Little did they know this would not be the last time.

The Volunteer movement had been reorganised into two groups, the Rifle Volunteers and the Artillery Volunteers, each with their own Drill Hall. The Rifle Volunteers built their Drill Hall in York Road in 1867 while the Artillery Volunteers built theirs off Nelson Road Central in 1880, on an open area later known as Artillery Square.

Following the Army reorganisation of 1908, there were changes in the military forces based in the town. By 1914 the Volunteers had become the Territorial Force, liable for service anywhere in the UK but not abroad unless the members volunteered. The Militia had been dissolved and the Victorian Barracks on the South Denes, for many years the headquarters of the grandly-named Prince of Wales Own Royal Norfolk Artillery Militia, who had their officers' mess at the Assembly Rooms (today the Masonic Lodge), now housed a detachment of the Royal Field Reserve Artillery. The Artillery Volunteers had become the 1st Norfolk Battery, Royal Field Artillery (Territorial Force) and the Rifle Volunteers were G and H companies

The Army Barracks on the South Denes, built in 1855. The roadway at the bottom right is today Dickens Avenue, earlier known as Quarter Mile Road. The Corporation bought the land from the government in 1924 to build the houses and roads of the Barrack Estate.

Officers and Senior NCOs of the 3rd Volunteer Battalion, Norfolk Regiment in camp on the South Denes c1907. This was transitional period for the army, hence the variety of uniforms worn by men of the same regiment.

of the 5th Battalion, The Norfolk Regiment and B Company (Cycle) of the 6th Battalion, The Norfolk Regiment.

The only fixed defence to protect the town at this time was an obsolete gun battery on the South Denes, originally designed to defend the harbour entrance. The Government had proposed to build a new battery in 1905 but, when the council declined to make a contribution of £1,000 towards the scheme, it was abandoned.

From 1900 Germany had begun to build up a naval fleet to challenge the Royal Navy's supremacy of the seas and the balance of power began to change. Previously any encounters with an opposing force would have meant an enemy had to pass through the Dover Straits, now there were German forces to the north. The Channel coast was protected against any attack, but the increasing threat was along the East Coast, where there were vulnerable and unprotected commercial ports. The closest naval base to Great Yarmouth was some distance away at Harwich.

The Royal Navy had its first submarines in service in 1903, primitive in design and very experimental. Development, however, was fast, encouraged by rising German sea power and by 1908 the fourth development of submarines, the C-class, was in service. These boats had petrol engines, were prone to explosive fires due to the inflammable fumes and lacked any internal dividing bulkheads. The living conditions for the crew of 16 were dreadful: they slept where they could and had no washing or toilet facilities. Armed with two 18-inch torpedo tubes, this class of submarine could travel at 8 to 10 knots on the surface but had a limited range when submerged. Despite these drawbacks there was never a shortage of sub-mariners to serve in them.

The port of Great Yarmouth had been no stranger to visits from these early submarines in the years leading up to the war. In May 1908, four C-class submarines were in port when two were caught by the strong tide and collided with Haven Bridge, providing an interesting spectacle for the townspeople. In July 1910, six submarines plus a destroyer arrived for a short stay and the following year there were four visits by a total eighteen submarines. On one occasion HMS *Thames*, a cruiser that had been converted into a submarine depot ship, anchored in the Roads while six C-class submarines entered the port. There were visits by one submarine in 1912, eleven in 1913 and nine in May 1914.

The implications of the German airship programme made the

Three C-class submarines, from their Harwich base, moored at the quayside c1908. These early submarines were frequent visitors to the port in the pre-war years.

Sunday 8 May 1908. Two C-class submarines, C5 nearest the bridge and C2, both caught by the tide against the Haven Bridge.

Admiralty think seriously about aircraft and airship development and, in 1912, the Royal Flying Corps was formed, with a naval wing, the Royal Naval Air Service. A chain of air stations, all within easy flying distance of each other, was established around the coast for use by aircraft then known as hydro-aeroplanes. In February 1913 a five-acre site on the eastern side of the South Denes was leased from the Corporation at a rental of £2 10s (£2.50) per acre per annum. The site complied with most requirements of an air station; the water frontage was suitable for launching 'hydro-aeroplanes' from slipways on the beach and there were mooring facilities nearby in the harbour for the boats needed to assist the planes. The Denes were considered suitable for land planes despite the fact that they were narrow so that they could only take off and land in a north-south direction and the Norfolk Pillar was an obstruction.

The station was commissioned on 15 April 1913 with 3 officers and 5 naval ratings with a headquarters established at 25 Regent Street, the men finding their own lodgings in the town. A hangar was built and the first land bi-plane, a French designed Maurice Farman Longhorn, No. 69, arrived from Hendon at the end of May and in June the first motorboats, *Margurite* and *Quest,* arrived. By July the station had four aircraft, three of them seaplanes, one of which was a Short Seaplane, No. 20. In July the Union Jack emblem carried on the main-planes and fuselages of all RNAS machines was replaced by a design of blue, white and red concentric rings. In November 1913 a new ferry was provided from Baker Street to convey workers and RNAS personnel across the river. The ferry closed in 1919.

In July 1913 a Caudron G.II, a two-seater biplane attached to HMS *Hermes* was at Yarmouth preparing to take part in Royal Navy manoeuvres. The *Hermes*, the parent ship for the Aeroplane and Airship Section of the Naval Wing of the RFC, had been fitted with a 100-foot long ramp in preparation for one of the first attempts to launch an aeroplane off a ship.

At this time Britain was a wealthy nation but industry was in decline. It was a land divided by class and wealth although new welfare reforms were improving the conditions of the working-class. There was still much poverty in the country and, at the beginning of 1914, industrial action by thousands of workers was threatening to paralyse the country. In Ireland, the conflict between the unionists and nationalists appeared to be leading that country into civil war as the British government prepared to introduce a new Home Rule Bill. Protests by the suffragette movement were becoming increasingly violent, not only in London but locally. In Great Yarmouth, they were considered responsible for the fire that destroyed the Britannia Pier pavilion on 17 April. The holiday industry was looking forward to a successful season and the herring industry, after having experienced record catches the previous year, was looking forward to a repetition. These two industries were the lifeblood of the town, the economy and the livelihood of most of the inhabitants depending on them. Unknown to them the second half of the year was to become a disaster.

In Sarajevo, on 28 June 1914, Archduke Franz Ferdinand and his wife were assassinated by a Serbian nationalist. This started a chain reaction throughout Europe and Britain moved into an alliance with Russia and France. On 3 August the British Foreign Secretary pessimistically said, "The lamps are going out all over Europe. We shall not see them lit again in our lifetime." The following day Britain declared war on Germany after Germany had entered neutral Belgium. In the last few hours of peace Prime Minister Asquith, full of foreboding, was quoted as saying, "We are on the eve of horrible things."

Before and after. The Britannia Pier pavilion was destroyed by a fire said to have been caused by Suffragettes on 17 April 1914. A new pavilion was built within a few weeks and opened on 6 July 1914, only four weeks before war was declared. Catlin's Royal Pierrots were to perform for the remainder of the season, despite the war.
The suffragettes stopped their militant action and demonstrations during the war years.

ON LAND

One of the first signs of war to be seen in the town were the armed guards, provided by the Territorial Force, which appeared outside the Coastguard Station on Marine Parade and the new Post Office in Regent Street the day after war was declared. The Coastguard Station had become the living accommodation for many of the men at the air station and the Post Office telegraph service was an important means of communication for the military authorities.

Also, on the second day of the war, men of the Territorial Force were mobilised, the 5th Battalion going by train to their HQ at East Dereham and the 6th Battalion to Norwich. Large numbers of men reported to the York Road Drill Hall to sign up and 'join the colours'. Also called up straight away were men of the Royal Naval Reserve; these men reporting to the Custom House before making their way to Southtown Station, cheered on by a large crowd of relatives, friends and well-wishers. Between two and three hundred Caister men were notified they were wanted for the RNR but many were away fishing in Scotland.

The men of the Royal Field Artillery returned early from their annual camp at Colchester and were quartered at the Nelson School (now St George's), the local horses hired for the camp stabled in neighbouring premises. On 8 August the Battery moved to camp at Spixworth, with almost every man volunteering for foreign service. After several months training the men embarked in November 1915 from Southampton for Le Harvre. One of the ships, the *Lydia*, was skippered by a Yarmouth man, Captain Darnell. These Yarmouth men, and their horses, were to see service in France, Egypt (1916), Palestine (1917) and Jordan (1918).

13

A public meeting was held at the Corn Hall, in Howard Street, to encourage more men to volunteer for military service. A sense of patriotic duty and national pride encouraged thousands of men across the country to come forward. Initially men were accepted if aged between 19 and 30, subject to a medical but, by the end of August, the upper age limit was increased to 35, or 45 for ex-soldiers. The local recruitment office was the Royal Artillery Barracks at the south end of town, although any police station would also accept recruits. In September a meeting was held at the Hippodrome to encourage more volunteers to sign up. There were now over 1,200 men from the town enlisted in the Army or the Navy. An urgent appeal was made for horses, desperately needed at the Front, and anyone with a suitable horse was asked to take it to the stables at the racecourse on the South Denes. Here it would be inspected and, if suitable, be purchased 'for the use of the country'.

As the country was now at war the Sword of Justice, part of the town's regalia, was unsheathed. This followed a long tradition dating back to at least the beginning of the eighteenth century; the sword remaining unsheathed when used on all public occasions until after a declaration of peace. This tradition is possibly unique to Great Yarmouth, the sword not put back in its sheath until July 1919.

A recruitment drive on Feathers Plain, Gorleston, in 1914 by the 5th Norfolk Regiment. The banner reads 'Wanted 300 recruits'.

In the autumn of 1914, lighting restrictions came into force, requiring minimum illumination to be used. This resulted in the trams not running along the Marine Parade after dark, although later this restriction was amended to allow them to run until 9.30 p.m. The following January it was ordered that all lights visible from the sea to be extinguished between half an hour after sunset and half an hour before sunrise. From September 1915 further restrictions stopped all trams from running after 7 p.m. but, to relieve reported hardships, the trams to Caister were allowed to run until 9.30 p.m.

The Easter Fair of 1915 was allowed to open on Thursday to compensate for early closing on Friday and Saturday due to the lighting restrictions and the refuse destructor, on Caister Road, was not allowed to burn after 8 p.m. All kerbs and crossings at street corners were whitewashed to assist pedestrians. From July 1915 all licensed premises had to close at 9 p.m. and the military authorities prohibited any form of photography or sketching within two miles of the coast.

The popular belief that 'the war would be over by Christmas' proved to be far from true although at the beginning, when large sea battles were expected, there tended to be a light-hearted attitude, as illustrated in a letter, sent home from a Yarmouth man serving on board the cruiser HMS *Blanche* in October 1914. He wrote:

> I am merry and bright, looking forward to seeing you all, by
> Christmas, as I am sure they will not last long once the Germans
> come out to meet us. We will break them up altogether. We on
> board are all getting fed up waiting for the day to come when
> we will meet them.

With no radio to listen to (the BBC did not begin broadcasting until 1922) newspapers and cinema newsreels were the only source of information for the general public. The local papers, the *Mercury* and the *Independent*, carried brief accounts of the progress of the war but press censorship severely limited their reporting. No mention was made of any military activity in the town or any references made to the air station or the naval base. Each week a Roll of Honour was published, listing men from the town who were wounded, missing or killed on service. The 'Letters Home' pages, although heavily censored, from serving soldiers to their family and friends, gave some indication as to the progress of the conflict and the hardship being endured by the soldiers. In September 1915 the *Mercury* published an album of photographs of 1,000 Yarmouth men 'Serving their King and Country on Land and Sea'.

In 1915 there was still great pressure on men to volunteer. Appeals were made during performances at the cinemas or theatre and in a letter in the Parish Magazine that year the Vicar wrote:

> There still remain a small number of unmarried and healthy men who have not volunteered their services, but are waiting for compulsion to be exercised. We trust that they will consider their position. Compulsion is certain to come...there should be no unmarried young men left in the streets that are physically fit and not employed in work for the country.

Newspapers regularly printed cartoons such as this to encourage young men to volunteer for military service.

The mobilization of troops was now in full swing as men were moved to war stations and anti-invasion positions along the coastline; others were prepared for service abroad.

The government encouraged local authorities to let any able-bodied young men enlist in some form of war service. This had a great effect on the police service, the transport system and the post office, older and less skilful men having to be recruited to fill the vacancies. In 1915 it was reported that a shortage of postmen meant there would only be three deliveries each day. As the war continued women joined the workforce and there were, for the first time, female conductors on the trams. The council told their employees that, if mobilised, they would be reinstated on their return and their wages or salary would be made up during the enforced absence.

Under the National Registration Act of July 1915, everyone between the ages of 15 and 65, living in the town, had to register their name, place of residence and other details at the Town Hall. They were then issued with a registration card. National Registration finished in 1919 but, when introduced in 1915, it helped pave the way for conscription the following year.

In January 1916 the Military Service Act was passed, conscripting all single men between the ages of 18 and 41. In May, when Lord Kitchener called for 300,000 recruits to form his New Army, a second Act was passed which extended the conscription to married men in that age group. By the time the war had finished over 7,000 men from the town, volunteers and conscripts, served in the Army or the Navy. The St. George's Men's Service, one of several such organisations run by the churches in the town, saw over 400 of their members join the forces, over 50 of them not to return. Like many similar organisations, St George's sent a weekly newsletter to all their serving members, wherever they were in the world.

The monthly newsletter being produced for serving members of St George's Mens Service, to keep them in touch with home. Mr Whitehead (centre) is seen here printing the newsletter at his home, 78 Wolseley Road.

Two photographs of the Great Yarmouth Volunteer Training Corps being inspected outside the Royal Aquarium on 28 February 1915. At the top are the men in the Volunteer Cyclist company. Membership of the VTC was restricted to those over the age of 38 years and who were not eligible for service in the Regular or Territorial Forces. In the cyclist company men had to provide their own bicycle.

Many men objected to being called up for military service for a multitude of different reasons, some on moral grounds but many others because of business commitments or dependant relatives. To voice their objections, they had to appear before a local tribunal held at the Town Hall, presided over by the mayor. Each week the cases were reported in great detail in the local paper, some objectors receiving delayed call-up, some having their appeal rejected and others, who were successful in their appeal, being directed to perform other types of war work. Men employed at home on war service were issued with official triangular 'On War Service' badges, to be worn on civilian clothes to protect them from the Order of the White Feather. In 1918 the Town Clerk, Mr W Edgar Stephens was awarded the OBE for his services as Clerk to the tribunal. At the same time the supervisor at the telephone exchange was given an OBE for courage and devotion to duty during air raids and bombardments.

Advertisements were placed in local papers for volunteers to act as Special Constables. Their duties included guarding buildings, patrolling the streets and giving warnings of air raids. Men too old to join the regular army joined the Volunteer Training Corps. This was

intended to mobilise those in reserve occupations or otherwise exempt from military service and by February 1915 the membership had passed 500. Volunteers were organised into patrols and guarded railway lines, bridges and other locations considered as 'sensitive'. The Great Yarmouth Volunteer Training Corps later became the 1st and 2nd Battalion, The Norfolk Volunteers, using the Winter Garden for drill in the afternoon and evening. A miniature rifle range was built under the Wellington Pier for the use of the military and also the general public. The latter were urged 'to learn to use a rifle so that in an emergency every man can do his duty in smiting the foe with lead'. There was another miniature range at the rear of St Peter's Plain, used by men of the Essex Regiment, and another on the Britannia Pier.

VTC Badge

In many parts of the town there were groups of ladies affiliated to the War Workers Association, making mittens, socks, mufflers and a large range of other items in great quantities for soldiers at the Front. They also made bandages and garments for hospitals in France, Italy and at home. By 1916 there were 400 members and the town was divided into five districts. That year they made 10,000 items. In February 1917 a new depot opened at 6 South Quay, the Mercury reporting 'Here ladies who have any spare time on their hands will be welcome, and where they can do some very useful work making bandages and dressings for our wounded'.

In 1915 there was a shortage of meat, followed the next year by sugar. In 1917 the Cultivation of Lands Order was issued, requiring any spare land to be used to cultivate food, mainly potatoes. Several sites were identified in the Borough including 120 acres of Corporation owned marsh which they agreed could be broken up and planted for potatoes and 'other substantial food stuffs'. Other sites included undeveloped building plots in Gorleston and Southtown and many small pockets throughout the town including the flowerbeds in the Wellington Gardens. By April a total of 22½ acres of private land was also under cultivation and land at the South Denes Racecourse had been divided up into allotments. Fish had now become an important food source and the 1917 fishing season, although severely restricted, was an important one. The military, in conjunction with the railway companies, ensured an efficient distribution of fish from the port to inland markets.

SUPPLIES OF MEAT.

In view of the increased demands for meat by the British and French Armies and of the relative shortage of vessels equipped for the conveyance of meat from overseas, the Board of Trade wish to call the attention of the public to the great importance of restricting the consumption of meat with a view to economising the national supplies and avoiding an excessive increase of price.

BOARD OF TRADE.
20th May, 1915.

By 1918, following a sustained U-boat campaign, during which thousands of tons of shipping carrying food supplies had been sunk, shortages were becoming more acute. In January, all the meat shops in the town announced they would only be open Thursday, Friday and Saturday each week and customers would only be allowed ¼ of their normal supplies. In February, rationing was introduced and the Ministry of Food issued ration books, which had to be registered with a preferred retailer. The first items to be rationed were sugar, tea, fats, butcher's meat and bacon. This was something the British housewife had not experienced before and the complicated system, particularly for meat, caused great concern and confusion. There was special provision for Jewish people to apply, on religious grounds, for vegetable oil in lieu of lard. The ration for one person for one week was 1 pound of uncooked (butcher's) meat, 6 ounces of butter and/or margarine, 2 ounces of lard, 4-8 ounces of bacon and/or ham, 8 ounces of sugar, 1½ ounces of cheese and 1½ ounces of tea. Meat came off ration in 1919, butter in May 1920 and sugar by the end of that year.

America had stayed neutral during the early years of the war but eventually entered the war on 6 April 1917. During 1918 they sent thousands of troops to fight in France. To mark Independence Day on 4 July 1918, a party of American troops visited the town to play two games of baseball at the Wellesley. A band met them at Vauxhall Station and the 600 troops marched to the town hall where they were given a reception. Banners proclaiming 'Welcome America' hung outside the town hall and across Regent Street.

INDEPENDENCE DAY
☞ THURSDAY, JULY 4th. ☜
American Troops Have decided to Celebrate This Day in Yarmouth.

They will arrive at Vauxhall Station at 12.50 and *THE MAYOR will welcome them outside the Town Hall at 1.15.*

A PROCESSION will be formed, headed by the
BAND of the 2nd Vol. Batt., Norf. Regt.
(by permission of Lieut.-Col. C. J. WILTSHIRE and Officers) and will proceed via Regent Street, Regent Road, and Marine Parade North, to the **WELLESLEY RECREATION GROUND**, where *TWO GRAND*
BASE-BALL MATCHES
will be played, commencing at *2.30.* Admission—*6d., 1s., and 2s.*

Proceeds to Local Charities.   The BAND will Play.

☞ The MAYOR invites residents and occupiers of premises on the line of route to *Decorate their Premises and Display Bunting,*

In the autumn of 1914 there was widespread fear of **INVASION.** Stories of German atrocities in Belgium scared the British public and 'invasion fever' took hold. Trenches and barbed wire defences were put in place along the coast of Norfolk, Suffolk and Essex. Guns were brought in to defend the beaches, parts of which were covered in barbed wire entanglements. Trenches were dug on Gorleston cliffs and in the gardens near the Britannia Pier and coastal defence was entrusted to the Cycle Battalions. In August 1916 a young boy on holiday in the town wrote home to his mother describing his holiday, saying:

> There are hundreds of ships lying off here and all along the
> front is [sic] trenches and earthworks. There are no gardens
> along the front now; everything is taken by the army.
> We went to Caister…hardly anyone to be seen except soldiers.

On 6 February 1915 the Mayor, Councillor David McCowan, issued instructions to every household as to what they should do in the event of bombardment or invasion. The notice stated that people should not go into the streets but keep in their cellar or on the ground floor of their home. If there was a hostile landing and a necessity to leave the town, all vehicles must travel by Caister Road and those on foot to proceed to the Acle New Road. People and vehicles from Southtown and Gorleston were to use the road to St Olaves via Bradwell and Ashby. People leaving the town should provide themselves with food and warm clothing and be prepared to move off the roads into adjacent fields, should the road be required for troop movements. Dykes on the Southtown marshes had been bridged for safety, if or when that route would be needed for evacuation

Many troops were brought into the town including the 4th Battalion Essex Regiment and men from the Middlesex, Shropshire, Cheshire and Monmouth Regiments. Some men of the Essex Regiment were billeted in property on the corner of Wellesley and Sandown Road but hundreds of other troops were billeted in private houses. The military paid the householder 9d (equivalent to £1.80 today) per man per day. Later in the war, empty houses were taken over as billets, the military paying half of what the rent was before the war. Many of these houses were empty because, when husbands had gone into military service,

Men of 'E' Company of the Essex Regiment, on the steps of their billet,
3 Brandon Terrace, on 3 December 1917.

A group of soldiers stand guard outside the Sailors Home (now the Tourist Information Office) on Marine Parade.

A 'posed' off duty picture of men of the Essex Regiment enjoying a drink at the Earl Beaconsfield, North Denes Road.

the wives and children had left the town to stay with relatives.

Following the Zeppelin attack in 1915 two 18-pound anti-aircraft guns were deployed to the town, one placed on the South Denes by the Nelson Monument and the other slightly closer to the harbour mouth. A Royal Naval Anti-Aircraft Mobile Brigade unit had been established with machine guns and searchlights mounted on Rolls Royce armoured cars. These vehicles were intended to protect the coast against the threat of Zeppelin raids but were based at Newmarket. A single 4.7 inch gun was installed on Gorleston Cliffs to protect the harbour entrance. This was midway between Clarence Road and Park Road and consisted of a magazine, two crew shelters and the gun mounted on an open platform. In 1918, the gun was replaced with a 15-pounder with another 15-pounder installed at Caister. The coastline from Mundesley to Yarmouth was patrolled by an armoured train, running along the M&GN line. This train had two 12-pound naval guns and a machine gun mounted on wagons with an armour-plated locomotive located in the middle. Although the train patrolled the line as far as Yarmouth Beach Station until the end of the war it did so without ever firing its guns.

In 1916 pillboxes were erected to defend strategic positions against any advancing invading army. Just outside the town two hexagonal pillboxes were built either side of the Acle Road and two round  pillboxes were built on the north and south walls of Breydon Water. The pillboxes on the Acle Road (above) still exist, one of the few surviving reminders of the Great War. Flood defence earthworks now cover the pillboxes on the Breydon wall.

The first half of the 1914 **HOLIDAY SEASON** had been a great success. The August Bank Holiday weekend saw the resort were full of happy holidaymakers but, within a few days, hundreds had quickly left the town, despite assurances from the council that they were safe. Over £700 was spent on advertising the town in the Midlands and North, while the railway companies were encouraged to continue with excursion trains. All national newspapers carried notices that the seaside was still safe despite the rumours circulating to the contrary. The *Daily Chronicle* said 'Public confidence should at once be established in the safety of visitors to the East Coast pleasure resorts'. Despite these assurances, the holiday industry was to have a difficult time for the remainder of the war years, leading to great hardship for those whose lives and incomes depended on it.

Although there was restricted access and barbed wire defences along most of the beaches, the section from Sandown Road to the Wellington Pier was clear and could be used during the summer season, with certain restrictions. For the 1915 season all beach stalls had to be removed by 7 p.m. in July and 6 p.m. during August and no bathing was allowed after 4 p.m. For the 1916 and 1917 season the corporation only leased sites on Gorleston beach, nothing was allowed on the Yarmouth beach. The Gorleston facilities were mainly for the benefit of local residents and the large numbers of military personnel billeted in the town, visitors being few in number.

The sudden effect the war had on the holiday industry can be seen from the August attendance figures for the Corporation-run Wellington Pier. On Sunday 2 August 12,000 people passed through the turnstiles but the following Sunday, after the announcement of war, the figure was down to less than 3,000. An announcement in the local paper on 22 August said 'The Piers Committee have unanimously decided to carry on their programme as usual, and trust their endeavours will receive the same generous patronage and support of both visitors and inhabitants'. Military bands, boxing tournaments and military concerts took the place of the usual concert parties. For the 1915 season, the General Manager tried to engage The Vagabonds concert party, but so many of its members were of military age that they were unable to appear. Roller-skating continued in the Winter Garden but only during the day owing to the lighting restrictions. The VTC and the Special Constables also used the Winter Gardens for drill practice.

The Britannia Pier was able to continue throughout the war almost as normal, with concert parties during the summer season and Sunday concerts throughout the year. Both piers, however, had to comply with the lighting restrictions that limited some performances to afternoons only. No doubt the large number of troops billeted in the town in part compensated for the lack of holidaymakers.

The Royal Aquarium closed in September 1915 because of the lighting restrictions and the curtailment of the tram service. All productions were transferred to the Theatre Royal in the centre of the town where the weekly programme of plays, drama, revue and musical comedy continued. The Royal Aquarium came under military occupation for the next three years, reopening as a theatre in August 1919.

Circus at the Hippodrome finished after the 1914 season and did not begin again until 1920. In 1915 there was film and variety entertainment for a few weeks but the building then closed, reopening in September 1918 with more film and variety.

The Gorleston Pavilion becoming a Naval and Military Social Club. It did not reopen as an entertainment venue until 1919. Another club for servicemen, the Yarmouth Army & Navy Club, was set up at the Dene Side Wesleyan Lecture Hall.

Cinemas had become a very popular form of entertainment, transformed in 1914 by actors such as Charlie Chaplin, who made his film debut in February that year. In the early weeks of the war telegrams, containing the latest war news, were sent to the Gem, Empire and Coliseum cinemas for immediate showing on the screen during each performance. The Pathe and Gaumont newsreels then became an

YARMOUTH
HIPPODROME

Sole Proprietor and Director,
Mr. GEO. GILBERT.
Ring Master ... MARQUIZ DE GONZA

WEEK COMMENCING

MONDAY, Aug. 10th, 1914

3   TWICE DAILY.   8

L. F. DURELL'S Company in a
Musical

AQUATIC REVUE

"HOIST YER SLACKS!"

Latest Songs.
Latest Ideas.
Latest Dresses.
Punting Ladies.
Swimming Ladies.
Singing Ladies.

In which 30 highly trained Ladies and Gentlemen Artistes will appear. No cost has been spared to make this Spectacle the finest yet seen in Yarmouth.

—— AND A FULL ——

Circus and Variety
Programme,
Including

The 5 Whiteleys.   Hinton and Wootton. Mr. Powell. The Bros. O'Brien.   De Lilo and Metz. Dan Gregory, Count Floydd, and

DOODLES

Twice Daily at 3 & 8.   Doors open half-an-hour previous.   Early Doors at 2.15 & 7.15, 3d. extra to all parts.   Booking Office open at the Hippodrome daily where stalls can be booked. Children under 10 years Half-price to all parts.

PRICES:

Stalls.   Pit & Prom.   Gallery.

1/6   1/-   6d.

Smoking allowed in all parts of the building. NOTICE.— No Goods are to be supplied without a written Order signed by the Manager.

The Regent Theatre when it opened on 26 December 1914. The performances usually consisted of films with two or three variety acts appearing twice during the evening. The theatre had a small orchestra to accompany the silent films and remained open throughout the war years.

important source of war news for the general public and, from 1917, the War Office issued propaganda war films in the newsreel format. The Gem closed in February 1915, not reopening until September 1918. The Empire remained open throughout the war. A new cinema, the Regent, opened on Boxing Day, 1914 and the following year, on Easter Monday, the Central Cinema in the Market Place opened. In Gorleston the Coliseum continued with film and variety while Filmland, in Beach Road, which had opened in July 1913, was enlarged in 1915 to cope with the increasingly large audiences.

Although the 1915 August Bank holiday brought large crowds to the town for a short period the general lack of seasonal visitors, combined with the great reduction in the herring fishery, brought severe hardship to many people. The Borough Council, in 1916, declared they were on the verge of bankruptcy due to loss of income from council run enterprises such as the trams, which had recorded a large drop in passengers, and the Wellington Pier, combined with the inability of local residents to pay their rates. A fund, known as the Canadian Fund, at first provided by the Canadian government and later supplemented by the British government was set up to 'give financial relief to East

Coast Watering Places suffering from wartime restrictions and lack of summer visitors'. By the end of 1915 this fund stood at £250,000 and boarding house keepers and others who were wholly or mainly dependent on the holiday season for their livelihood were eligible to make a claim. The maximum grant available was set at £30 but this could be increased in exceptional circumstances to £100. More help for those in financial distress came in 1917 when the town received £14,500 in Government aid, with an additional £33,250 from the Canadian Fund.

The town was to suffer three **COASTAL BOMBARDMENTS** during the course of the war. On Tuesday 3 November 1914 the first attack on this country by a hostile fleet for 250 years was aimed at Yarmouth and Gorleston. Four battle cruisers and four light cruisers of the German High Seas fleet carried out the first so-called 'terror raid'

The guns that bombarded the town on 3 November 1914. These 11 inch guns are mounted on the German battle cruiser SMS *Von der Tann*, one of the ships in the fleet that took part in the November raid. The ship, of 21,000 tons, had eight such guns mounted in four twin turrets. With a range of 12 miles they could fire 670 pound shells. The *Von der Tann* later took part in the Battle of Jutland and was finally scuppered at Scapa Flow in 1919.

against a virtually undefended east coast. The Mercury reported that 'many people had their breakfasts quite spoiled…about 7 o'clock their slumbers were ruthlessly disturbed by the rattling of windows and sounds like distant thunder. There was a pell-mell rush towards the sea afoot and on bicycles'. Estimated to have been at least 10 miles offshore, and not visible from land, the enemy ships fired volleys of shells, all falling in the sea, short of the beach. The German warships had taken their bearings from the St Nicholas lightship, which had, unbeknown to them, been moved further out to sea. It appeared that people at the north end of the town thought it was a fight between German ships and British ships while at the opposite end of the town, people watching from the sea front and the high ground at Gorleston, feared an invasion was imminent. Soldiers were called out to man roadblocks in the town and women and children wept in the streets, all fearing the worst. A newspaper reporter later said 'This was our first taste of what actual warfare means'.

On hearing the exploding shells three submarines belonging to the Harwich 8th flotilla that were in the harbour at Gorleston at the time, quickly put to sea. Meanwhile HMS *Halcyon*, an old patrol gunboat based at Lowestoft, was only four miles from the cruisers when the shelling began and was attacked and damaged by the German battleships. The *Halcyon* was able to relay the position of the enemy by wireless, allowing two destroyers, HMS *Lively* and HMS *Leopard*, which were patrolling in the area, to close in. *Lively* set up a funnel smoke screen, allowing the *Halycon* to escape. The German ships, realising they had been detected, quickly retreated, one leaving a trail of floating mines in its wake. One of the submarines, *D.5*, which was running on the surface, struck one of the floating mines and sank in less than a minute. A nearby drifter saved two officers and two men who were on the bridge of the submarine but 20 submariners were lost. The survivors were landed at Lowestoft and Yarmouth where one was taken to the Crossley Hospital. Despite submarines and destroyers being deployed from other ports the German battleships escaped. At the time of the bombardment there were no serviceable aircraft at the air station, their only machine was undergoing maintenance. Following this bombardment eight centres for giving emergency first aid to persons injured on such occasions were set up in the town.

The **SECOND BOMBARDMENT** happened in the early hours of Tuesday 25 April 1916 when shells fell on Lowestoft, Yarmouth and Caister. A Zeppelin had been reported overhead during the night but had been repelled by aircraft. At 4.24 a.m. the bombardment began, with shells falling on the Denes near Newtown causing large craters but no damage. One shell fell on the Corporation nursery near the destructor on Caister Road, making a huge crater, the debris from which blocked the main road. Another shell hit the Empire cinema on Marine Parade, also damaging the shopping arcade next door. (A brass plaque was later placed on the wall of the Empire to mark the event, but this disappeared many years ago). Many shells fell short into the sea while others landed on the marshes beyond the town. Shed roofs on the Fishwharf were damaged and a fish store owned by Smiths Dock Company was destroyed, barrels, swills and thousands of fish being thrown into the air. In Gorleston shell fragments hit houses in Trafalgar Road West. The bombardment lasted about twenty minutes and it was estimated over 100 shells were fired but no warships could be seen; only the flashes from the guns as the salvos were fired. Although four people were killed and twelve injured in Lowestoft during the same bombardment there were no casualties in Yarmouth or Gorleston. Many residents of the town, who had initially gathered along the sea front when the noise of the guns was heard, quickly dispersed when shells began to fall in the sea, deciding that the safest place would be the marshes to the west of the town. When the shelling had stopped, almost the entire population left in the town came out to see what damage had been caused and children were quickly out collecting shell fragments, some still hot, later to be sold as souvenirs. Some of these souvenirs no doubt still exist in the town. Submarines from the port, two E-class, three H-class and one V-class, had been ordered to sea on patrol in anticipation of the raid. Only one of them however sighted the enemy and dived to attack but could not get within range. Two of the submarines had to dive when they were mistaken for German submarines and attacked by aircraft from the Great Yarmouth air station. Despite attempts by British warships to engage the enemy the German fleet managed to escape.

The Rector of Caister, whose rectory was on the cliffs with an uninterrupted sea view, recorded this event in the parish register. He noted:

Eight 12-inch shells [this may be an exaggeration as other reports give the number as 3 shells] fell in the parish shortly after 4 a.m. but caused no loss of life. After this date the church tower was used as a Naval Observation station with a crew in attendance night and day until the end of the war.

Another resident of the village reported that the 'terrific cannonade about 4 a.m. had brought many people to the streets and within a short time the village was practically evacuated'. The residents made their way to the higher ground in the west and saw that a huge cloud of smoke hid Yarmouth.

The **THIRD BOMBARDMENT**, the last, took place on Monday 14 January 1918 during a heavy rainstorm and gale. It started at 10.55 p.m. with the German warships firing a star shell to illuminate the town. In about eight minutes 50 shells fell on the town, killing a husband and wife, Mr and Mrs Sparks, who were in bed when the roof of their house fell in and two seamen on a vessel in the harbour. Another eight people were injured and admitted to the General Hospital. A number of houses suffered damaged roofs and many windows were blown in. Only three or four shells fell on Gorleston, one finishing unexploded on a couch after striking the corner of one house, lifting the roof off another, passing through a brick wall and then through another house. Bad weather prevented any aircraft from the air station from taking off, none of the submarines were sent out and the monitor ship, *Roberts*, did not retaliate.

The Edward Worlledge school log recorded the next day that 'many boys late, searching for shrapnel. Sixteen shells fell within a 400 yard radius of the school'.

NORFOLK MUSEUM SERVICE-TIME & TIDE MUSEUM

Until the 1970s there was a plaque, with brass lettering, (left), in the pavement in St Nicholas Road recording where one of the shells from this bombardment fell. The plaque is now in the Norfolk Museum store.

32

The first **AIR RAID** on this country occurred on 19 January 1915, and Great Yarmouth was the target. In the months leading up to the war the townsfolk had become used to seeing aeroplanes from the air station flying over the town and no one even considered there could be a threat from the sky. Most people were barely aware that Germany had developed giant airships capable of crossing the North Sea. Little did they know that Great Yarmouth was to be the first place in the country to experience at first hand the terror of an air raid by a Zeppelin, the first time in history that the ordinary citizens of this country were attacked while still in their homes by an aerial bombardment. Many people were confused as to whether the raider was an airship or an aeroplane, later confirmed as the former. The number of bombs dropped by the Zeppelin varies in different reports. Contemporary newspaper reports claimed eight, but later descriptions of the raid have said eleven or twelve. Some bombs were dropped very close together and confusion arose as to whether these were single or multiple explosions.

It was a cold, foggy, wet night when three airships of the Imperial German Navy set out from their base at Hamburg to attack ports along the East Coast. One airship returned to base after experiencing mechanical problems but the remaining two, after crossing the North Sea in mid-winter conditions with their open control cars and primitive navigational aids, arrived off the Norfolk coast shortly before 8 p.m. The L4 crossed the coast at Bacton and then headed north towards King's Lynn. The L3 crossed the coast at Happisburgh and headed south towards Great Yarmouth.

L3, the Zeppelin which dropped the first bombs on British soil on 19 January 1915, seen here at its German base. With a top speed of 50 mph and a crew of 16 this airship could carry up to 1,430 pounds of bombs.

33

After nearly colliding with Martham church tower, the airship was seen overhead by the master of the Rollesby Workhouse. The first explosive bomb to land on British soil was dropped from the Zeppelin onto a field near Ormesby water works. The next, an incendiary bomb and the first bomb to fall on the town, landed on the lawn of a house in Albemarle Road, not far from Beach Railway Station (now the coach park). Some reports claim a fire-basket was dropped at the same time, over Norfolk Square to illuminate the town.

The next, an explosive bomb, landed at the rear of 78 Crown Road but failed to explode. It is possible that this bomb split into two just before impact, as two pieces were later found a few yards apart. The next day the remains of the bomb were dug out and taken to the Drill Hall in York Road and put on view to a large number of interested sightseers.

The next bomb to drop, another explosive bomb, caused the greatest damage and resulted in two deaths, the first in the country caused by an aerial bombardment. It fell in St Peter's Plain blowing out the front of Mr Ellis's house, St Peter's Villa, now recorded as the first house in Great Britain to be damaged by a bomb. Nearby property was also extensively damaged including the workshop of Mr J Pestell, a builder and undertaker. Windows in York Road, Lancaster Road, Dene Side, King Street and St Peter's Plain were broken. Masonry and stained glass windows were damaged at St Peter's church. The *Mercury* reported, 'The scene on St Peter's Plain was one of considerable ruin'. The two people killed were Martha Mary Taylor, a 72-year-old lady who lived at 2 Drake's Buildings, her body found outside Mr Pestell's office and Samuel Alfred Smith, a 53-year-old shoemaker of 44 York Road, who had been standing outside his shop when he was struck by several bomb fragments. A local doctor, Dr Leonard Lay of Alexandra Road, later removed a splinter from a soldier injured in the explosion and became the first surgeon to operate on an air-raid victim. The *Yarmouth Independent* printed some interviews with eyewitnesses, the following from William Storey who lived at 17 St Peter's Plain.

> I and my wife and sister, a baby two years old, and one nine
> months old, were in the back room when there was a tremendous
> explosion. The gas went out and we were left in darkness.
> You know what women are in these times. They are all shrieks!

34

I couldn't find a match or anything, and everywhere I moved
I stumbled over something. When at last we got a light we found
the door off and the windows blown out and everybody's house
near a wreck. In Mrs Scott's house next door some of the doors
are absolutely knocked into matchwood, and how she and her baby
escaped is a miracle.

On the opposite side of the road, where Mr Pestell's building was
wrecked, Mrs Pestell recounted the following.

We were sitting in the living room when my daughter exclaimed
'Mother I hear an airship. Aeroplane I ejaculated but she insisted
it was something different, and upon my going to the door I
heard something coming along just like a motor car. Then
something came down with a wizz. Looking up I saw over the
church an airship shaped like a cigar, and I rushed upstairs. One
of the children cried 'Oh mummy, come !' and I thought the
place was on fire for smoke was coming out of the room. I
snatched the children up; they were covered with plaster from
the fallen ceiling. Afterwards my husband went out, and almost
immediately stumbled over a woman whom he found to be dead.

The next bomb fell into stables in Garden Lane owned by Mays the
butcher, landing harmlessly in the hay next to a pony. The next day
this bomb was also displayed in the Drill Hall.

An incendiary bomb then fell in Southgates Road, exploding outside
the First and Last public house. The next day some fragments of the
bomb were exhibited on the bar, the landlord seizing the opportunity to
draw in customers.

Beeching's South Dock was hit next as an incendiary bomb hit the
dock gates but then sank into the river, narrowly missing the local
drifter *Mishe Nahma* (YH 494). The damage to the gates caused the
dock to flood.

An explosive bomb struck Trinity Wharf but failed to detonate and
fell into the river. The next bomb fell at the foot of the salt-water tank
behind the Fishwharf. It exploded and did considerable damage,
bursting a water main and shattering windows in nearby buildings. The
Fishwharf Refreshment Rooms public house suffered most damage,
the landlord, Joseph Steel, giving a graphic account to the local paper

Above: the scene of devastation in St Peter's Plain following the bomb attack. Below left: Mr Ellis standing outside his house. A blue plaque has now been placed on this house recording the event. Below right: windows in St Peter's church damaged by the blast. .

Local residents gather outside the bomb damaged New Royal Standard in St Peter's Road. Note the news boys, ready to sell their papers.

Soldiers with part of the outer casing of the Zeppelin bomb that had failed to explode after falling at the rear of 78 Crown Road, near Gordon Terrace.

They are seen here outside the York Road Drill Hall where two bombs were exhibited the day after the raid.
The bombs were later taken out to sea and detonated underwater by explosive charges.

saying the blast had raised the roof of the building and the force of the explosion caused a picture hanging in his drawing room 'to turn round and face the wall'.

The steam drifter *Piscatorial,* moored in the river at the end of the Fishwharf, was damaged by the next bomb. The last bomb, an explosive bomb, to be thrown out of Zeppelin L3 landed on the South Denes at the rear of the racecourse grandstand, near the Crossley Red Cross Hospital, leaving a large crater and blowing out windows in many houses on the Gorleston side of the river.

Two overhead telephone routes were brought down by the bombs, leaving about 100 subscribers out of order, including the Naval Air Station. The day after the raid, fragments of bombs were exhibited in several shop windows in the town and two unexploded bombs were on public view at the York Road Drill Hall. The bombs that dropped on the town that night were small compared to later Zeppelin raids but two people had lost their lives and total cost of the damage to both private and corporation property was assessed at £2,500. Martha Taylor was buried at Caister on 22 January and Samuel Smith was buried the following day in the Yarmouth cemetery.

This was not the only Zeppelin attack on the town. On 24 April 1916 an airship was driven off by gunfire from anti-aircraft guns and on 2 September 1916 a single airship dropped several bombs on the marshes, causing no damage. Examples of the incendiary and explosive bombs dropped by the Zeppelin can be seen in the Time & Tide Museum war gallery.

Damage caused by the bomb that fell on the Fishwharf, close to the salt-water tank. The bomb caused considerable damage to buildings nearby, including the pub, the Fishwharf Refreshment Rooms.

Samuel Smith's grave in the Yarmouth cemetery.

A German propaganda postcard showing how a Zeppelin had supposedly attacked and set fire to the Yarmouth Town Hall, the Rathaus.

Many such postcards were produced after attacks on British towns and cities making false claims as to the success of the air raids.

In the first few weeks of the war it was realised that many more **HOSPITALS** and medical care would have to be provided. Within a few days of war being declared the Admiralty announced that wounded naval personnel would be landed at Yarmouth for treatment. The north bay of the covered Fish Market was made available as a suitable landing place for the wounded. Twenty beds were made available at the Sailors Home, eighteen at the Nurses Home and more at the General Hospital and Gorleston Hospital.

At a public meting, held to appeal for beds, furniture and any hospital equipment, Sir Saville Crossley (of Somerleyton Hall) offered to equip and maintain a hospital for as long as it was required. To accommodate this, a large building on the South Denes was offered by Mr James Bloomfield, the fish merchant and herring fleet owner. This hospital was established within a few weeks and became known, in various reports, as Lady Crossley's Red Cross Hospital, the Crossley Hospital or the Bloomfield Hospital. Beds were supplied by the town's department stores, Palmers, Arnolds and Bonnings. Among its first patients were 11 wounded Belgians, part of a group of 74 brought to the town from Colchester for convalescence. The Crossley hospital had 50 beds and a fully equipped operating theatre. Lady Crossley was the matron and there were five nurses.

By October wounded soldiers from the Front began to arrive back in this country in large numbers. Over sixty auxiliary hospitals were set up in Norfolk, in private houses or suitable commercial buildings, run by the Red Cross and the Order of St John, staffed mainly by members of the Voluntary Aid Detachment. This organisation had been formed in 1909 to support the Territorial Army by providing medical assistance in times of war and to supply assistant nurses, ambulance drivers and cooks. The soldiers sent to these auxiliary hospitals swapped their khaki uniforms for simple blue clothes and a red tie. Known as 'hospital blues' these clothes provided the wounded soldier with a distinctive sign of status, and indicated that he was a man from the Front.

A small Red Cross hospital had been set up in a private house at 47 Marine Parade, at the southern end of Britannia Terrace (now an amusement arcade). On 20 March 1915 this was closed and the staff and patents moved into a large house, lent by the executors of the late Mrs J. Hurry Palmer, on the corner of Kings Road and Nelson Road,

A patient arriving at the Seafield Red Cross Auxiliary Hospital, King's Road, in the 'town ambulance' which had been provided in 1915 by Mr Allen, a local wine and spirit merchant. The ambulance attendants, and the nurses, are members of the Voluntary Aid Detachment.

The Voluntary Aid Detachment nurses at the Seafield hospital in 1915. In the centre is Mrs C Orde, Vice President of the Great Yarmouth branch of the British Red Cross Society.

known as Seafield. This larger Red Cross hospital had capacity for 25 cases. Among the early patients were some of the wounded from the battle of Neuve Chapelle, transferred from the Lakenham Military Hospital in Norwich. The battle had taken place in north-west France from 10 to 13 March and had resulted in 7,000 British casualties.

The War Office only covered the cost of food for these hospitals, all other expenses had to be found from Red Cross funds or donations. Throughout the war the hospital was supported by local fund raising events and donations of food and equipment by local people. In 1915 Mr S J Allen, a well-known local wine and spirit merchant, gave his motor vehicle to be adapted as an ambulance, the first motor ambulance in the town. This was driven by members of the VAD and used to transport the wounded from Southtown station to the hospital. Patients were given free admission to many places of entertainment in the town, including the Theatre Royal and the Central Cinema.

Although Seafield was sold to a new owner in September 1917, the hospital continued until March 1918, then all the patients and equipment was transferred to the nearby Melton Lodge, on the corner with Marine Parade. The Auxiliary Red Cross Hospital Melton Lodge closed on 17 January 1919. During the war the Seafield and Melton Lodge hospitals treated a total of 730 servicemen. In 1923 Seafield House reopened as a convalescent home for Salvationist bandsmen.

The nursing staff at Melton Lodge Red Cross Auxiliary Hospital in 1918 after they had been transferred, with all the patients, from Seafield.

The General Hospital on Deneside treated many servicemen as well

42

as civilians throughout the war. In 1917 those receiving treatment included 33 naval personnel, 83 from the army, 11 airmen, four neutral sailors and one prisoner of war. Other hospitals in the town included the York Road Drill Hall where 40 beds were made available and the Town Hall with 50 beds. The roof of the Royal Naval Hospital, at that time used as a Naval Asylum with over 100 patients, was painted with red crosses on white grounds.

In October 1914 £400 was raised in the town to provide an ambulance to be used at the Western Front. The vehicle was a 20 hp Vauxhall, fitted with an ambulance body able to carry four stretchers. A plate attached to the vehicle read: 'Presented by the residents of Great Yarmouth and District'. The vehicle was sent to France, driven by a local man, Mr B. Ward, who had previously worked for the motor firm belonging to Messrs. H.G.St. John Ltd. The *Independent* printed a letter from Boulougue Sur Mer in France in which Mr Ward described the conditions the ambulance was working under. Part of the letter reads:

> I thought it might interest you if I gave you a rough description of the kind of work the ambulance is doing out here. The day's work starts with reveille at 6.30, wash and then for breakfast bacon, bread and jam, to which we do good justice. We then proceed to the cars, our convoy is split up into three sections and each one is told off [sic] to clear a field hospital or dressing station. The wounded are brought back to a clearing hospital which is cleared every day, the trains taking them to the base. The guns are booming day and night, they never seem to stop but one gets used to it after a while. The roads are awful, the mud sometimes up to the axle and they are usually decorated with shell holes. The towns and villages out here are smashed to pieces.

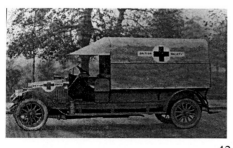

This photograph of the Yarmouth ambulance was printed in the *Independent* with Mr Ward's letter.

FUND RAISING became essential to help pay for the war and the government appealed to the public to purchase war bonds or war saving certificates, portraying this as a patriotic duty. By 1917 war bonds had reached their third issue, paying 5% interest. War Saving Certificates and Victory Bonds raised a considerable amount of money, as did voluntary contributions from the general public. Schools and work places raised money by sales and many other schemes and, throughout the war, special weeks were allocated to particular fund raising activities.

In March 1916 there was a 'Warship Week' and the Blofield & Flegg area aimed for £120,000 to buy a Corvette. The first week in April 1918 was 'Tank Week', many places having a real tank on display. Norwich was able to raise over £1 million during the week, its tank having been brought by rail and then driven to the city centre.

Great Yarmouth was not allocated a real tank but, not to be outdone, the corporation improvised by converting one of its tram cars to look like a tank, giving it the number YH 777 to add a local connection with the fishing industry, seven being considered a luck number by many fishermen. The 'tram tank' stood on Hall Quay together with an aeroplane brought from the air station and the week raised £183,000.

The 'tram tank' and the aeroplane on Hall Quay. The mayor and official party are standing on the top deck of the tram.

44

After the war had finished money was still required and on 7 July 1919 two Victory Loan Campaign rallies were held. The first was at 11 a.m. on Hall Quay followed by another at 12 noon on Feathers Plain, Gorleston. Two Anglo-Russian cars were brought to the town as part of the rally to encourage people to attend and listen to speeches by the mayor, Alderman A. Harbord and the deputy mayor E. W. Worlledge.

PETER JONES COLLECTION

The Victory Loan rally, on Feathers Plain, Gorleston.

The **CLIFF HOTEL**, an imposing hotel standing high above the harbour on the Gorleston cliffs, had been built in 1898. In 1914 it became the headquarters of the Senior Naval Officer of the Naval Base, HMS *Kingfisher,* which had been established on the Gorleston side of the river. On Boxing Day 1915 fire broke out in one of the hotel bedrooms and, fanned by a strong south-west gale, the building was destroyed within hours, one of the biggest fires ever seen in Gorleston. The fire began at 9.15 p.m. and the limited resources of the local fire service, although assisted by many naval and military personnel, stood no chance of beating the flames. The port tug, the *George Jewson,* arrived and pumped water from the river up to the fire. No lives were lost and part of an annex to the hotel was saved although the belongings of the few visitors were destroyed. Military personnel guarded the ruins of the hotel after the fire, no doubt to protect the part

45

used by the naval authorities. The following August the licence was transferred to the nearby St. Edmund's boarding house.

The ruins of the Cliff Hotel the morning after the fire, guarded by military personnel.

On 11 November 1918, at 12.30 p.m., the mayor announced that the **ARMISTICE** had been signed from the balcony of the Town Hall to a huge crowd on Hall Quay. The macebearers and Town Clerk, in full regalia, accompanied him with the sword, still unsheathed. In the afternoon there was a parade through the town led by a band which was followed by the submarine men with fixed bayonets, a group of mounted officers, thousands of soldiers, a gun drawn by six horses and wounded soldiers from Melton Lodge. The mayor took the salute on Marine Parade as low flying aircraft threw down paper streamers and ribbons. In the evening, for the first time in four years, lights appeared in windows and on the streets. That evening the parish church was packed from wall to wall for a thanksgiving service, similar services being held in other churches and chapels throughout the town. In Gorleston, the Middlesex Regiment provided the music, marching up and down the street while people cheered and sang. In the harbour the ships were decorated with streamers and flags.

AT SEA

Four days after war had been declared, with anti-German feeling running high, a wooden German schooner, the *Fidcecia,* which had been loading oilcake at J & H Bunn's wharf, was seized to the surprise of its captain and crew. The ship was taken up river and berthed at Stonecutters Quay, with a naval officer and customs officials aboard. A few days later another German schooner, the *Theodor,* bound for Kings Lynn with a cargo of locust beans, was captured at sea by a British destroyer and brought into the Roads. She was then brought into port and moored alongside the *Fidcecia.* The crew of seven were taken to the Barracks and made prisoners of war. The *Theodor* was later towed to Lynn with a British crew on board to discharge her cargo.

On 19 September the Admiralty issued a notice about the removal of lightships. Five of the more distant lightships were brought into port, including the Dudgeon and Smith's Knoll, while those closer ceased to show their main light, only riding lights left on. The lighthouses at Winterton and Happisburgh stopped flashing and red navigation lights on the Sailors Home, Britannia Pier and Gorleston harbour were turned off. In June 1916 the Corton lightship was blown up by a mine. Five of the crew of seven were lost; the two survivors brought back to port by a naval vessel.

The Admiralty hired one of the port's paddle tugs, *King Edward VII,* only a few days after the war had begun. It left for Harwich with the usual crew on board who, only a few days before, had been taking holidaymakers on pleasure trips. The tug returned to Yarmouth in August 1919. The paddle steamer *Lord Roberts* was hired, with the name changed to *Earl Roberts,* for minesweeping duties from July 1916 until March 1919.

Many other vessels from the port, including local pleasure steamers, were involved in the war effort such as the *Yarmouth,* which became a tender to the battleship *Iron Duke* at Scapa Flow. The Admiralty took a large fleet of steel lighters, owned by Henry Newhouse and used on the river between Yarmouth and Norwich under the name Waveney & Yare Lighter Co. Ltd., in 1916 for war service on continental canals.

The tug *King Edward VII* leaving her berth near the Town Hall, taking holiday makers on a sea trip, just a few days before she was hired by the Admiralty for war service. With her crew the tug went to Harwich, not to return to Yarmouth until 1919.

A SUBMARINE BASE, a supplementary base to Harwich, was established at Yarmouth in August 1914 in response to increasing hostile activity in the area. At that time the Royal Navy had a total of 86 submarines, divided into nine flotillas. Four were used as patrol flotillas and five were for coastal defence. The nearest, the 8th flotilla, was based at Harwich and used for offensive patrols off Holland and Germany and defensive patrols off the East Coast. A C-class coastal submarine, from the 3rd flotilla at Dover, was brought to Yarmouth, soon followed by five more submarines. HMS *Adamant* was, for a short time, the depot ship until replaced towards the end of the year by HMS *Alecto,* under the captaincy of Cdr. Sir Leonard Vavasour. Depot ships, or mother ships, provided support, repair and supply services to their flotilla of submarines. The *Alecto*, which had a complement of 76, was moored at Bryant's Quay, at the south end of South Quay, opposite Friars Lane. This was to remain the submarine base until the end of the war. A wooden fence was erected to enclose the quay from the road with a gate at the northern end. Wooden and canvas workshops and accommodation for the crews were built on the quayside and in September British Petroleum installed two large fuel tanks on the quay for the submarines. Local engineering support for the submarines was provided by James Combes, engineer and smith, who had premises at 64 South Quay and at the western end of Row 143, almost opposite the base.

An aerial view of the submarine base on South Quay. HMS *Alecto* is moored at Bryant's Quay with one submarine alongside and three more further north. The road on the right of the picture is Friars Lane.

The submarine base with HMS *Alecto* in the background and workshops and accommodation units on the left of the picture.

49

HMS *Alecto*

For the duration of his stay in the town, the captain of *Alecto* did not stay on his ship but lived in a large house in Euston Road, a building that was later the Labour Club for many years. The Officers' Mess was established in a house on South Quay, opposite the base.

In October three E-class submarines, the largest wartime class, left the port to serve in the Baltic. The first coastal bombardment occurred in November and three Harwich submarines, *D.3, D.5* and *E.10* that were in the port and berthed at Gorleston, put to sea after hearing the rumble of gunfire from the German battleships off the coast. Because of the distance the submarines were unable to make contact with enemy but one, *D.5*, struck a mine and sunk with a loss of twenty members of her crew as described earlier. D and E-class submarines were larger than their predecessors and had diesel engines. The D-class had three 18-inch torpedo tubes and a crew of 24 while the E-class had five torpedo tubes and a crew of 30.

An H-class submarine (*H.5)* at the base on South Quay. In the background are the canvas and wooden workshops built on the quayside.

Wireless was still in its infancy in the early years of the war and was not fitted in the submarines. Their only means of communication when at sea was by carrier pigeons, each boat carrying a small crate of birds that were released to relay messages back to their base.

In January 1916 four H-class submarines from Harwich were permanently based at Yarmouth. These were submarines of American design and carried four torpedo tubes. The port now became the main base for the 8th flotilla, the Harwich flotilla renumbered as the 9th.

In April the second coastal bombardment occurred, the target being the Lowestoft minesweeping base and the Yarmouth submarine base. The submarines from Yarmouth were patrolling off the coast in anticipation of a raid but when it happened they were too far away to engage the enemy. Unfortunately they were then attacked by British planes, which had mistakenly identified them as German U-boats. Following this bombardment the submarine flotilla was reinforced by small coastal submarines moving down from the Firth of Forth. The Yarmouth flotilla continued with their patrol duties off the coast but does not appear to have been involved in any enemy action.

Submarine development had led to several new classes by January 1917 and the 8th flotilla now consisted of two F-class, five H-class and four V-class boats. The number of boats in the flotilla varied throughout the war and by June 1918 there were eight boats, four H-class and four V-class. By November this was reduced to six, four H-class and two V-class. The Yarmouth submarines carried out coastal patrol duties but when the third, and last, bombardment of the town happened on 14 January 1918 for some reason no submarines from the Yarmouth base were sent out.

In 1919 the *Alecto* base was cleared and Bryant's Quay was returned to the Port & Haven Commissioners. The quay was then taken over by the shipping company T. Small & Co. and used for their steamer service to Hull.

The submarines that had been based at Yarmouth during the war were as follows. *D.2, F.1* to *F.3, H.5* to *H.10, H.21, H.23, H.24, H.26, H.28* and *V.1* to *V.4*. Three submarines, *D.2, H.6* and *H.10* were lost while based at Yarmouth and *H.5* was lost while attached to another flotilla. Only four V-class submarines, to a Vickers design, were built. They proved unsuccessful for Navy purposes and were mainly used for training.

In 1916, following the second bombardment of the town, a **MONITOR SHIP,** HMS *Roberts,* arrived to reinforce the town's defences. Monitor ships were a class of warship neither fast or strongly armed, but carried disproportionately large guns. Among the *Roberts* armament were two 14-inch guns and she was recalled to Yarmouth from the Eastern Mediterranean waters. In addition to the 14-inch guns she had two 12-pounders, one 5-pounder and one 2-pounder.

The *Roberts,* a ship of 6,250 tons, built by Swan Hunter in 1915 and first named *Stonewall Jackson,* was moored on the Yarmouth side of the river, opposite the lifeboat sheds. An unusual form of camouflage was adopted when the ship was painted to look like a row of houses. The *Roberts* had the only searchlight in the town, used to illuminate Zeppelins as they came in from the North Sea. The tall fire control tower on the ship was yet another hazard for the aircraft from the air station trying to take off or land on the South Denes. Despite having all this armament and being brought to the town to defend it, the large guns on *Roberts* were only fired once, in practice, and on that occasion many windows on the Gorleston side of the river were shattered. At the end of the war the ship was moved to the Gorleston side of the river and most of her armament dismantled.

Ironically the **FISHING INDUSTRY** had had its most successful year ever in 1913 when record catches were recorded. The following year saw the outbreak of war and, from August, the Board of Agriculture banned fishing in the North Sea except during daylight hours and within sight of land. By October 1915 limited fishing was possible but now the previously lucrative German and Russian markets had disappeared. The naturalist Arthur Patterson wrote,'

> The fishing boats working out of Yarmouth in 1915 were of the older type, the Naval Authorities having taken over the pick of fleets at Yarmouth and Lowestoft, and laid a heavy hand on the fishermen themselves.

Admiralty restrictions on the areas that could be fished, the danger from mines and U-boats and the shortage of boats due to the number taken into Admiralty service severely limited the catches, as the following records show:

52

	English boats	Scottish boats	Catch in crans
1914	309	62	117,459
1915	55	144	120,122
1916	59	0	12,289
1917	49	209	77,782
1918	47	291	202,485

Most of the Yarmouth-owned drifters that did not continue fishing during the war years, or were not hired by the Admiralty for war service, were taken up river to Cantley, Reedham and Brundall where they were kept until the war had ended.

As the German attacks on convoys bringing food supplies into the country increased, the supply of locally caught fish became more important than ever. Throughout the war years however the fishing industry took a heavy toll. At first it was mines that destroyed the boats and their crews, such as in November 1914 when the two Yarmouth steam drifters *Copious* YH 370 and *Seymolicus* YH 846 were both lost with all hands. German submarines then waged war on the British fishing fleet, a U-boat surfacing among a group of fishing boats, ordering the crews to abandon ship and then placing an explosive charge in the fish hold. Nine Yarmouth registered drifters, not on war service, were lost during the course of the war. Two are mentioned above, the others, all sunk by German submarines, were:

Piscatorial	YH 297	Sunk 23 June 1915
George Baker	YH 537	Sunk 17 August 1915
Petunia	YH 576	Sunk 6 July 1916
Renown	YH 477	Sunk 28 July 1916
Twiddler	YH 779	Sunk 2 August 1916
Heather	YH 799	Sunk 24 April 1917
Primrose	YH 570	Sunk 18 May 1917

In the first weeks of the war the **YARMOUTH NAVAL BASE** was established. Destroyers from Harwich, the nearest major fleet base, had patrolled the vulnerable coast of Norfolk and Suffolk for several years. From the onset of war this patrol was increased and four destroyers patrolled off Yarmouth during the night, each morning returning to port to take on coal from a collier. The local paper reported how enthusiastically fifty volunteers from the port labour force helped load the coal to give the destroyer crews a rest.

When more bases were required along the East Coast one of the earliest to be established was the Yarmouth base, given the name HMS *Kingfisher*. An administrative headquarters was set up at the Cliff Hotel and the Royal Naval Barracks, with a store above, was at the bottom of Baker Street. Later a Naval Recruiting Office was established in Cliff Hill. In 1915 the Senior Naval Officer was H G Sherbrooke.

The Admiralty required small craft that could be used for minesweeping and anti-submarine work and in many fishing ports the local fleets were an ideal source from which to obtain these vessels, the skippers and crews called up for the Royal Naval Reserve. At Yarmouth a total of 184 drifters and 3 trawlers were hired by the Admiralty for various wartime duties, about two thirds of the local fleet. The boats were hired from their owners on a monthly basis, the payments ranging between £20 and £60 per boat per month. Over four hundred of Bloomfield's staff joined the colours and the Rector of Caister recorded.

> The fishermen of this parish, almost without exception,
> served in steam drifters on patrol service, the master
> of each drifter being given the rank of Warrant Officer.

Armed with 3-pounder or 6-pounder guns some boats served as minesweepers or escort vessels but the majority were used as net-barrier tenders in conjunction with anti-submarine nets. For these duties each drifter was equipped with 10 nets made of galvanized wire and having a mesh of 10 feet, the net floated by hollow glass balls. When laid in a line the nets stretched for about 100 yards and the boat drifted on the tide with them. Buoys were attached at intervals and if a submarine hit the net it would drag it away, the buoy being towed

The drifter *J.H.F.*, YH271, one of the many local drifters hired by the Admiralty for war service. The deck was reinforced to take the weight of the 3 -pounder gun seen at the front of the boat. Named after her owner, John Henry Fuller, this boat had been built in 1914 and was used by the Admiralty for net duties from July 1915 until 1919.

Two drifters moored at the Naval Base. In the background is the South Denes and the wireless aerials for the Air Station. YH 295 is the *Girl Kathleen*, used for net duties from October 1916 until 1919. Moored alongside is a drifter from Scotland, with an Admiralty number 265, also on war service.

along the surface giving away its position to the accompanying destroyers. A net of this type was laid in 1915 in the Dover Straits, designed to block the southern approach to the North Sea.

Later a more successful method was developed where nets, with mines attached, were permanently anchored in a long line, the mine damaging any submarine hitting the net. The drifters continually patrolled these net barrages, which were successful for a time, forcing the German submarines to reach the Atlantic by the longer northern route. In February 1918 the *W.Elliot*, YH 423, on net duty in the Dover Straits, was sunk by a German submarine. Eleven hands were lost and the skipper, J. Mair, was later awarded the DSC. One of the WRENS stationed at the naval base, Catherine Bennett, described her duties:

> The majority of women were doing mine-net work, others storekeepers and clerks. Net work involved splicing cables and ropes, attached to mines, to the nets which were then taken down to the quay where we helped load them onto the drifters.

By 1917 the Germans had overcome the net problem by keeping on the surface but only moving under cover of darkness. A new system of floodlights, deep minefields and massed patrols by up to 100 drifters was able to combat this, the submarines now forced to dive to avoid being seen, but then caught by the deep mine field.

A net barrage had been placed across the Adriatic to prevent German submarines reaching the Mediterranean. Of the 100 drifters sent to man this barrage, many were from Yarmouth. In 1917, the *Girl Rose*, YH 786, was among 14 drifters sunk by Austrian cruisers off Fano Island in the Adriatic. Another Yarmouth drifter, the *Floandi,* YH 973, was also attacked but the skipper, Dennis John Nichols, although wounded, stayed at his post in the wheelhouse and assisted in saving the more severely wounded of his crew. Skipper Nichols then took a small boat and, joined by engineman Charles Mobbs, plugged the holes in the drifter's side enabling her to reach port. For this he was later awarded the DSC. The wireless operator, Douglas Harris, sent and received messages until he was killed by a piece of shrapnel while writing in the log.

There were many such acts of bravery by the skippers and crews of Yarmouth drifters, such as an incident in June 1917 when HMD *I.F.S.,*

YH 188, skippered by Lieut. H. B. Bell-Irving RNVR encountered five enemy seaplanes and engaged them. One aircraft was destroyed and another attacked, the two pilots taken prisoner. The second seaplane sank while being towed to port and the other three planes escaped. In November Lieut. Bell-Irving received the DSC and bar at Buckingham Palace.

The Admiralty commissioned a number of new boats to be built in the port. Fellows shipyard built several although some were not completed until the latter years of the war, some too late to be used for war service. In 1917 a steel vessel, HMD *Dayspring,* was completed, followed in 1918 by the wooden vessels *Darkness, Daylight* and *Fireball.* In 1919 HMD *Elephanta* and in 1920 HMD *Belle Vue* were completed. The drifters completed in 1919 and 1920 had been ordered just before the war ended, so it had been too late to cancel them. Fellow's dry docks were also used throughout the war by the Admiralty for submarine repairs. Crabtree's yard was also involved, building a steam trawler for the Admiralty in 1915 and three steam tugs for the War Office between 1917 and 1918. Between 1918 and 1920 they also built five steel steam tugs for the Admiralty, with a sixth order cancelled. The landing stage for the Upper Ferry, on the west side of the river, was in the centre of Crabtree's yard. This had to be moved a few yards on a request from the Admiralty to make the yard more efficient.

A variety of vessels were stationed at the Yarmouth Naval Base including two old destroyers, HMS *Lively* and HMS *Leopard. Lively* was a B-class torpedo boat destroyer of 391 tons built in 1900 and *Leopard* was a three funnel C-class destroyer built in 1896.

Early in 1915, the *Queen Alexandra,* LO51, a RNMDSF mission trawler based at Gorleston, was withdrawn from serving the fishing fleet in the North Sea due to the mine peril and fitted out for the Admiralty as a Hospital Ship. When completed the ship was painted white with large red crosses painted on her superstructure and funnel. The mission depot provided off-duty facilities to personnel from the naval base including a specially built café.

Towards the end of 1917 the Admiralty explored the possibility of establishing a naval base on Breydon Water but after detailed investigation the idea was dropped.

The officers and crew of HMS *Lively*, one of the destroyers attached to the Naval Base. They are seen here at the base of the Royal National Mission to Deep Sea Fishermen at Gorleston. Here the personnel from the naval base were provided with off-duty facilities.

The RNMDSF trawler *Queen Alexandra* at the Gorleston base after being converted by the Admiralty into a hospital ship in 1915.

Of the 187 Yarmouth boats hired by the Admiralty during the war 17 were lost.

City of Liver- pool	YH 244	Mined 31.7.18
Frons Olivae	YH 217	Mined 12.10.15
G.S.P	YH 487	Sunk in collision 2.2.17
Girl Eva	YH 346	Mined 2.10.16
Girl Rose	YH 786	Sunk by Austrian cruiser 15.5.17
Hastfen	YH 93	Mined 24.9.17
Twenty Four *	YH 674	Mined 25.3.16
J.C.P	YH 767	Sunk in collision 22.3.18
John Robert	YH 708	Mined 1.12.19
Lerwick	YH 747	Mined in the Roads 27.3.16
Ocean Fisher	YH 345	Mined 16.6.18
Ocean Foam	YH 970	Sunk in collision 7.10.18
Ocean Plough	YH 792	Mined off Lowestoft 27.8.18
Piscatorial II	YH 762	Disappeared off Newhaven 29.12.17
Select	YH 577	Sunk in collision 16.4.18
W Elliot	YH 423	Sunk 15.2.18
Waveney	YH 745	Sunk 27.10.16

*This boat was renamed *Hilary II* when hired by the Admiralty.

The only Yarmouth vessel to become a Q ship (a decoy vessel) was the former mission smack *G. L. Munro*. Q ships were introduced due to the increasing activity of enemy U-boats in the North Sea. The gun was disguised as a deck housing or concealed under a tarpaulin or dummy hatch. At the start of the war the ship belonged to the Watts Naval Training School at South Quay and when war broke out was laid up in the harbour. Early in 1917 she was taken over by the Royal Navy, fitted out as a 'Q' ship, armed with a 12-pounder gun and placed under the command of Lieutenant Arthur Rickards, RNR. Renamed the *George L. Muir* she was then used to carry coal from Leith to Kirkwall in the Orkneys, bringing back cargoes of kelp to the Firth of Forth during the remaining years of the war. Whether or not she was successful in sinking any German submarine is unknown, but after the war she returned to Yarmouth and was laid up until eventually sold in 1926.

HMS *YARMOUTH* was a light cruiser, launched on 12 April 1911 from the yards of the London & Glasgow Co., and was the fifth Royal Navy ship to carry the town's name. The ship had visited the town in 1912 and, in August 1914, the council sent a telegram to the officer in command informing him that the inhabitants of the town wished the ship 'God speed, Honour and Glory'.

. HMS *Yarmouth* helped pioneer powered flight from warships. Many experiments had been carried out between 1910 and 1914 and *Yarmouth* was one of 22 ships fitted with a fixed platform, 36 feet in length, to enable an aircraft to take off. The fixed platform was later replaced by a revolving platform, allowing an aircraft to take off into the wind regardless of the direction the ship was travelling in. The returning plane had to ditch in the sea, often resulting in the loss of an airframe and engine and hopefully not the pilot as well. On 28 June 1917, Royal Naval Air Service Flight Commander F. J. Rutland took off in a Sopwith Pup from a platform mounted on the roof of one of *Yarmouth*'s gun turrets, the first such successful launch of an aircraft from a ship at sea in history. As well as being in the forefront of this new application HMS *Yarmouth* also claimed the only operational success against Zeppelins resulting from the use of aircraft launched from a ship. On 21 August 1917 the airship L23 was destroyed off the Danish coast by a Sopwith Pup N6430, launched from the ship. On returning to ship the aircraft ditched in the sea and sank although the pilot was saved. HMS *Yarmouth* was eventually sold for scrap in July 1929.

IN THE AIR

Towards the end of July 1914, the **ROYAL NAVAL AIR STATION** on the South Denes, together with the other RNAS coastal stations, was put on a war footing and ordered to prepare for coastal patrols. On the outbreak of war, the station had a complement of seven officers, two warrant officers and 40 ratings. A few ratings lived under canvas at the station but most were accommodated at the Coastguard Station (then known as the Coast Defence Station) on Marine Parade, which had been vacated by the Coastguard Service. Other air station personnel were billeted with local families and, later in the war as numbers increased men were billeted in hotels such as the Royal and the Victoria (now the Carlton) and at the Imperial Boarding House (now the Imperial Hotel). One pilot, Captain Marlow, wrote in his war diary 'We have been moved to the Royal Hotel, [from the Victoria] more comfortable at 8/6 [40½p] a day, special rate.' The men paraded in the yard at the CDS each morning and were taken to the air station by lorry. This caused problems for the corporation as the heavy traffic damaged the road surface, the borough surveyor claiming damages from the Admiralty towards repairs. On many occasions personnel from the air station were required to police the town, having to patrol, among other places, various entertainment venues. According to Captain Marlow it was not unknown for the duty pair to discard their armbands and gaiters under a bench on the pier and join the dancers. Due to some off-duty escapades by personnel of the RNAS the initials were often said to stand for 'Rather Naughty After Sunset'.

The site on the South Denes had been fenced in with corrugated iron and hangars and workshops were erected. On 14 August a system of three regular flying patrols began, at dawn, midday and sunset, covering the coastal area from the Wash to Southwold. Although these patrols were flown for the remainder of the year they were often

61

Above: The layout of the RNAS Air Station on the South Denes in 1918. The hangars and maintenance sheds are built along a narrow strip of land, with the open Denes behind for the land planes. Note the two slipways for launching the hydro-aeroplanes. Below: The wooden hangars at the air station.

These two views of the air station are taken from the scale model which can be seen today in the Flixton Aircraft Museum at Bungay.

limited by bad weather and the shortage of machines, meaning no enemy, either surface or air-borne, was seen. The limitations of wireless telegraphy at this time meant the planes relied on carrier pigeons to convey messages back to the station should they have to ditch in the North Sea and the only armament each plane carried was a .303 Lee-Enfield rifle, laid across the pilot's knee.

Following the coastal bombardment in November 1914, when no planes from the station were serviceable, more aircraft were sent to Yarmouth. When the first Zeppelin air raid occurred the following January, although three planes were serviceable, none was able to react in time.

Throughout the next two years there were many Zeppelin raids on this country, on most occasions the airships crossing the Norfolk coast before heading inland to London and other targets. Although machines from Yarmouth were now able to respond quicker, because the raids took place under cover of darkness, they had little success in attacking airships, unable to either see or hear them.

Take off and landing during the night for the land planes at Yarmouth could be difficult because of wind conditions and the obstacle of the Norfolk Pillar. Seven satellite night landing grounds were set up at Aldeburgh, Bacton, Burgh Castle, Covehithe, Holt, Narborough and Sedgeford. The Burgh Castle site, opened in 1915, covered 50 acres and had three hangars. Other sites had living accommodation, hangars and maintenance buildings. To aid night landings the sites used flares, fuelled with petrol or paraffin.

At any one time at least half the planes were out of service due to the shortage of spare parts but by August the number of planes had increased to 27 and submarine patrols had started. One of the pilots stationed at Yarmouth was Flight Sub-Lieutenant Egbert Cadbury, heir to the chocolate empire, who had joined the station in August 1915. A 22-year-old Cambridge undergraduate he had served on minesweepers before being appointed a commission in the RNAS. While stationed at Yarmouth he married Mary Phillips, daughter of the Gorleston vicar, the Rev. Forbes Phillips. Cadbury was decorated twice during his service at Yarmouth for destroying two Zeppelins. He lodged at a house in Kimberly Terrace, a building on which a blue plaque was fixed in October 2013.

Henry Allingham, who died in 2009 aged 113, described in his autobiography as 'Kitchener's last volunteer' was stationed at Yarmouth at the beginning of the war as an air mechanic. Henry flew as an observer on many occasions, including with Cadbury and described the planes as 'motorised kites, flimsy constructions of wood, fabric and wire, powered by an engine less powerful than a car. The instrument panel had six dials, there was a joystick and a rudder bar and to say they were unreliable is putting it mildly'.

On 13 April 1916 King George V made a visit to the town, arriving by car from Lowestoft. After inspecting the Naval Base at Gorleston he travelled to Yarmouth where large crowds lined Hall Quay, Regent Street and Regent Road to see the royal car pass. At the Air Station he inspected a line up of machines and was introduced to their pilots, including Cadbury. The king was shown the Sopwith Schneider seaplanes armed with Lewis guns, darts for puncturing Zeppelins and small bombs. The king returned to London by train from Southtown Station. Although the visit was reported in the local paper, no mention was made of his visits to the military instillations.

When the second coastal bombardment occurred on 25 April 1916, the station was better prepared and one plane, flown by the station CO, was able to attack the German warships while another two planes attacked the accompanying Zeppelin airships, but again without any real success. A searchlight had been installed on the monitor ship *Roberts*, moored in the river, but the next nearest searchlight was at Lowestoft. Yarmouth planes now patrolled a 130-mile stretch of coast from Kings Lynn to Felixstowe. The German airship raids were now reaching their height and on 3 September fourteen airships attempted an attack on London. The air station was alerted and Cadbury took off at 10.25 p.m. in pursuit of one but although he sighted it in a searchlight beam from Lowestoft, he lost it in the cloud at 6,000 feet.

By now considerable advances had been made in aircraft armament. A synchronising mechanism allowed a Vickers machine gun to fire directly through the rotating blades of the propeller and the rear seat observer carried a Lewis gun. Incendiary bullets were able to penetrate and set fire to an airship and new bomb release gear carried more effective bombs. Wireless telegraphy had a much longer range and a compass, adapted from a nautical instrument, aided navigation. Parachutes had been invented but were never issued to RNAS crews.

A Maurice Farman Longhorn biplane, the first plane to arrive at the air station in May 1913. First built in 1912 by the French aircraft designer Maurice Farman this two seater had a Renault 'pusher' 70 hp engine and had a maximum speed of 59 mph.

Many of the early aircraft stationed at Great Yarmouth were seaplanes, launched from a slipway and recovered on the beach. This Short seaplane, No 20, was one of the first to be stationed at the air station and is seen here being recovered on the Gorleston beach in 1913.

In July 1916 more land was required to expand the air station and the Admiralty informed the council that they were taking over another 21 acres of the South Denes under the Defence of the Realm Act. Some anti-submarine patrols were now in the air for up to six hours and night flying from the station increased. There were 46 aircraft available but during the year several planes and officers had been lost. One of these was Flight-Lieutenant Graham DSO, killed when his Short seaplane failed to attain enough speed on take off and dived into the sea from 200 feet. The bombs he carried exploded and he was killed instantly. Incidents like this were unfortunately common.

On 28 November 1916 aircraft from the Yarmouth station had their first real success. Seven Zeppelins had raided Yorkshire, the Midlands and the North and one, the L21, was sighted returning over Norfolk in the early hours of the morning. Several planes were sent up, including one from Burgh Castle flown by Flight Lieutenant Cadbury. Although he was not the only pilot to attack the airship it was Cadbury who was credited with setting it on fire. It crashed in flames into the sea 10 miles off Lowestoft, leaving no trace except a patch of oil on the surface. Three pilots were decorated for this mission, Cadbury receiving the DSC. By the end of 1916 the station had 31 aircraft and 29 pilots.

Bad weather in the first months of 1917 severely curtailed any flying. In April the station's first flying boat, a Curtis H.12 twin-engined, No 8660, arrived from Felixtowe with another, No 8666, the following month. These were American flying boats, bought by the Navy. No 8666 to become the most famous flying boat in the service. With a greater range and better armament the flying boats could search for airships off the Dutch coast, each one carrying three or more Lewis guns and four 100lb bombs. Their first success came in May when flying boat 8666 shot down a Zeppelin off Terschelling, earning the station the distinction of having the first flying boat to destroy an enemy airship.

By August the station had 35 landplanes, 23 seaplanes and two flying boats. Hickling Broad had by now been taken over as an emergency landing ground for seaplanes and flying boats. To improve the access to the broad the sails on Chapman's drainage mill, which stood on the edge of the broad, were removed.

This model of a Sopwith Baby shows the colour scheme and markings used for the planes at the Yarmouth Air Station.

By 1917 the Zeppelins were loosing their effectiveness and the Germans introduced a new phase of aerial attacks, large Gotha bombers, which attacked in daylight. The first attack was on London in May and the following August the 'Yarmouth Striking Force' came into being. Flying Horace Farman, Pup and Strutter aircraft this force was intended to attack hostile aircraft rather that airships. The Yarmouth force was, however, unsuccessful as none of the new aircraft came within their patrol area.

On 31 March 1918 the Royal Naval Air Service and the Royal Flying Corps were merged into a single service, the Royal Air Force. Aircraft at the air station were divided into three squadrons, the land planes becoming No. 212 Squadron, with Captain Cadbury in command, the boat flight becoming No. 228 Squadron and the Short and Schneider flight No. 229 Squadron.

On 5 August 1918, Bank Holiday Monday, the last Zeppelin raid on this country took place. Five airships, led by Captain Peter Strasser, head of the German Naval Airship Division aboard the L70, the latest and finest of the German fleet, led the attack that was targeted on London. The airships made their approach over the east coast and were spotted by lightships. Coastal defences were alerted, including the Yarmouth air station, which sent messengers into the town to summon the officers and men. Cinemas flashed a notice on the screen informing all air station men to report at once. One of the officers alerted was Major Cadbury, who had been at the Wellington Pier Pavilion with his wife Mary, who was singing at a charity concert being held in aid of the Mission to Seamen. When he was called at 8.45 p.m. he is quoted as saying:

> I roared down to the station in an ever-ready Ford, seized scarf, goggles and helmet, tore off my coat and took a running jump into the pilot's seat. I knew, that, given a reasonable amount of luck, I should certainly destroy one, if not three of the intruders.

Aircraft had been scrambled from several airfields including Yarmouth. Cadbury was flying a De Havilland DH4 with Captain Robert Leckie as his air gunner in the back seat. Cadbury found the L70 and was able to attack, the phosphorous bullets from Leckie's gun tearing a great hole in the airship, which plunged into the sea off North Norfolk, a blazing wreck. Although he then chased other airships the altitude and cold conditions meant he was unable to attack, returning to a landing ground at Sedgeford, soon after 11 p.m. Cadbury and Leckie were both awarded the Distinguished Flying Cross for their actions that night. This was to be the last time hostile Zeppelins crossed the coast of East Anglia, the last air raid of the war.

The last engagement of the war for the Yarmouth air station was on 16 September 1918 when a patrol of two flying boats and a land plane met five German seaplanes off Zeebrugge. One of the enemy seaplanes was presumed to have been shot down as it was seen to be on fire, its destruction was however not confirmed

By the end of the war the Yarmouth air station had a complement of 80 officers and 900 men. Never intended to be permanent, the station was now wound down, although mine spotting patrols continued for some months. The RAF informed the Council that they would stop all landings on the Denes from spring 1919, and the lease would be terminated on 25 March 1920. The aircraft and stores were dispersed to other stations and, by the beginning of 1920, only one officer and six rating were left to oversee the final closure, which happened at the end of January. The last of the stores were loaded onto a lighter, the keys handed over to a civilian caretaker, and the air station was closed.

Some of the ground crew at the Air Station in front of a Sopwith Pup.

The funeral procession of Flight Sub-Lieutenant G W Hilliard passing along St Peter's Road, in September 1915. Hilliard was the first war casualty of the RNAS at Yarmouth.

On attempting to land at the satellite night landing ground at Bacton, following a two-hour patrol, he misjudged the distance and landed in an adjacent field. The undercarriage of his plane collapsed and the bombs he was carrying exploded, killing him instantly.
Incidents like this were not uncommon.

The Coastguard Station on Marine Parade as it would have looked when taken over for the accommodation of men serving at the air station. Built in 1858 the buildings were demolished in 1964 to make way for the Tower complex, now the Atlantis nightclub. The wooden tower to the left is one of the many beachcompany lookouts that were along the sea front.

Officers and men from the air station gather in the courtyard of the Coastguard Station before a Sunday church parade. Each day lorries took the men from here along the Marine Parade to the air station .

Although not now required by the RAF the Civil Aviation Dept considered part of the site could, in the future, be needed for the development of flying boat traffic and some of the buildings should be retained. This however was never to happen, the South Denes was only used for occasional pleasure flights into the late 1920s.

The three large hangars, three small hangars, offices and sheds, engineer's shop and general store and the fence were eventually removed. Until recent years three brick buildings that were once part of the air station survived. A large building close to the beach was, for many years, used by the Corporation as a store, while two other smaller buildings, said to have been barrack huts, became toilet blocks for the caravan site established on that part of the South Denes in the 1950s.

A cigarette case made with metal from the L70 and engraved with Cadbury's signature can be seen in the Great Yarmouth Time & Tide Museum war gallery. After the war Egbert Cadbury left the service and became managing director of Cadbury Brothers Ltd. He died in 1967. Also in the museum is a wooden propeller, possibly from one of the flying boats stationed at Yarmouth.

In May 1915 an **AUXILIARY PATROL BASE** was set up in the harbour at Bollard Quay, Southtown. Its purpose was to develop an effective means of defence against the increasing airship raids on the country. Zeppelins liked to cross the coast at dusk, using the cover of darkness and cloud but there was little chance of aircraft being able to climb to the Zeppelin's altitude to intercept them before the darkness hid the airship from view. The answer was to patrol well out to sea, near the Dutch coast, allowing the seaplanes to waylay the airships at dusk and dawn. The naval base provided the boats while the air station provided the aircrew and mechanics. The Yarmouth base covered a part of the North Sea known as 'area X', from North Norfolk to North Holland and South Suffolk to North Belgium (except the Harwich local area).

The mother ship was named HMT *Kingfisher*, a 304-ton steam trawler that had been requisitioned by the Admiralty as she neared completion at Crabtree's shipyard in early 1915. The vessel was being built for Portuguese owners and was to be hired fnamed *Alcyon*. Three more trawlers, *Cantatrice, Jericho* and *Sir John French*, were hired from Hull and Grimsby and, armed with 12-pounder and 6-pounder guns, were fitted with a platform to carry an aircraft. The patrol base was at Bollard Quay, renamed Aviation Quay. By July 1915 a fifth trawler, *Christopher* from Hull, had joined the patrol fleet. From January 1916 the Sopwith Schneiders were gradually replaced by Sopwith Baby aircraft. The trawler *Cantatrice* was sunk off Yarmouth on 5 November 1916 after hitting a mine, the crew of 18 and the pilot of the Sopwith Baby were all lost. On 30 March 1917 the *Christopher* was lost in a similar incident.

HMT *Kingfisher* operated from June 1915 until May 1916 but the other trawlers only operated with a seaplane for brief periods between these dates. From December 1916 to July 1917 two torpedo gunboats, *Halcyon* and *Dryad* were added to the fleet and in March 1916 a Humber paddle steamer, *Brocklesby*, was converted to carry two seaplanes on deck and joined the trawlers at the Yarmouth base, patrolling off the Dutch coast until March 1917. Flt Sub Lt E Cadbury flew from *Kingfisher* on four occasions in 1916 and the previously mentioned veteran of the Great War, Henry Allingham, went to sea on *Kingfisher* and *Brocklesby* as an air mechanic, later saying that he preferred the paddle steamer as, when on the trawler, he had to sleep in the fish hold.

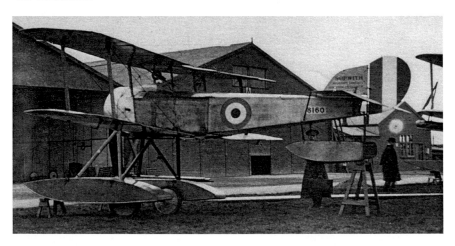

This Sopwith Baby operated from HMS *Brocklesby* on anti-submarine patrols in 1916. It is fitted with wheels as well as floats.

Although many patrols were carried out, when conditions were calm enough, no Zeppelins were ever sighted by aeroplanes from the Yarmouth patrol base. The failure to achieve success was not through the lack of skill and enthusiasm of the pilots; it could only be put down to bad luck and bad visibility.

A first hand account of experiences in flying from *Brocklesby* and *Kingfisher* were recorded in the war diary of Captain Augustine Marlow, a pilot posted to the air station in 1916. He writes:

> I have been out in the North Sea on board our little seaplane
> carrier Brocklesby with the Schneider seaplane on deck
> waiting for reports of Zepps [sic] or subs. There were two
> of us, Davis was the other pilot, and we were out for two or
> three days but no enemy action. The Brocklesby is an old
> paddle steamer. After I had to go out on my own except that I
> took 'Mick' my Irish terrier with me for company, and it
> was a different boat, the Kingfisher, a trawler. A crane on the deck
> is used to hoist the seaplane with pilot and deposit us on the
> water and back again on board afterwards. One submarine
> was reported but I failed to find it and when I found the trawler
> again afterwards it had difficulty in making contact with me
> as the wind and waves kept slewing me round.

When not required for patrols, the aircraft, Sopwith Schneider and Sopwith Baby seaplanes, were winched off the decks of the boats onto the northern end of Aviation Quay and then taken to a large wooden hanger across Southtown Road, just into Boundary Road for maintenance and storage. Local people, seeing the aeroplanes lined up on the quayside, called this Aeroplane Quay.

The paddle steamer *Brocklesby* was handed back to her civilian owners in June 1917, having been found unsuitable for work in the North Sea. The trawler *Kingfisher* was handed back to her intended Portuguese owners in early 1919 under her original name *Alcyon*. The name Kingfisher was transferred to another local vessel, the Yarmouth drifter *Adele,* until the auxiliary patrol base finally closed on 9 September 1919.

From 1915 the Auxiliary Base carried out much experimental and development work in the use of aeroplanes flying from naval ships, work which eventually led to the aircraft carriers of today.

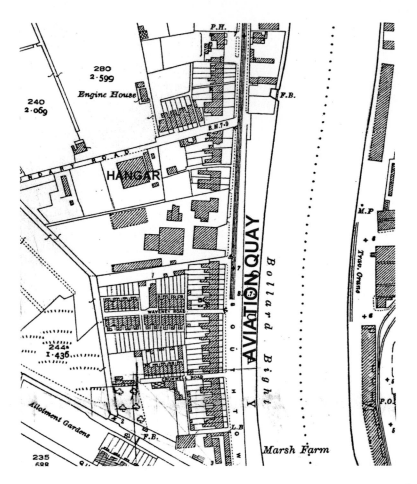

This 1928 map shows the position of the aircraft hangar in Boundary Road in relation to Bollard Quay, which had been renamed Aviation Quay during the war. Local people, seeing many aircraft on the quay called it Aeroplane Quay.

The hangar, of wooden construction, was 80 feet square and after the war was used by the United Bus Company as a depot, taken over in 1931 by the Eastern Counties Omnibus Company Ltd.
It was in use until 1938 when it was destroyed by fire.

THE POST-WAR YEARS

The erection of **WAR SHRINES** had begun in 1915, the long lists of missing and killed resulted in an outpouring of grief, expressed in the erection of shrines in honour of fighting men. These shrines were designed to commemorate those who had gone to war, rather than those who died in the war and would have memorials erected at a later date when war had finished. In November 1916 the town's first war shrine was unveiled by the mayor at the eastern end of Victoria Street, near St Paul's Mission Hall. This shrine recorded the names of 63 men from Victoria Street, Estcourt Road, Maud Terrace and Mission Place and 61 men who were relatives of residents of those streets.

In Cobholm, a close-knit community where many men had joined the colours, another shrine was built, in 1917, in the south-west corner of the playground of the Cobholm Infants School. This was idea of a schoolteacher, Miss Barnaby Smith, and was unveiled at 3 p.m. on 10 May that year, amid much publicity and with a ceremony attended by the mayor and representatives from the Navy, Army, Air Services, local volunteers, nurses from the Seafield Hospital and the bands of the Essex Regiment and the Volunteer Training Corps.

The shrine consisted of a cross, surmounted on an octagonal oak base, on which were eight wooden panels, hand painted with the names of 730 men from 'Cobholm and district' who had responded to their countries call in the general war'. Of the names on the panels 53 had already died in service when the shrine was completed, 44 in the army and 9 in the navy. Designed by local architect Arthur Hewitt and constructed by Beech of Deneside the wooden structure was not to

Cobholm War Shrine.

THIS SHRINE WILL BE
:: **UNVEILED** ::
BY
HIS WORSHIP THE MAYOR
(ALD. E. W. WORLLEDGE) IN STATE, ON
THURSDAY, May 10th
AT **3** P.M.
DEDICATION SERVICE
BY THE VICAR
(ARCHDEACON C. LISLE CARR).

By kind permission of COL. W. C. SHEPHERD
and COL. C. J. WILTSHIRE,
:: **THE BANDS** ::
OF THE
Essex Regt. & V.T.C.
WILL BE IN ATTENDANCE.

The unveiling of the Cobholm War Shrine by the mayor on 10 May 1917. Built in the corner of the school playground the shrine was removed in the 1960s.

The tank that was given to the town in 1919 as one of the 'spoils of war'. Seen here soon after its arrival from Beach Railway Station on 3 December, with the Mayor, Councillor Bayfield, and other civic dignitaries now standing on the top, before it was driven onto its plinth near the Town Hall entrance.

stand the test of time and when taken down in the 1960s the wood had rotted and the names were unreadable, the shrine was beyond saving it was subsequently destroyed.

Towards the end of 1918 the Council, together with other councils, had appealed to the government to release essential building supplies so that 're-decoration and repairs rendered necessary by the serious dilapidations of properties caused by the military occupation' could be carried out in anticipation of an influx of visitors for the 1919 holiday season. The following January, having received no reply, the War office was asked again to vacate all properties by 31 March as most were 'in a lamentable state'.

In December 1918 a German submarine, UB28, which had been towed by a tug from Harwich, was brought into the harbour and moored alongside the *Alecto*. For one month the public were, for an entrance fee of 6d, able to view from the quayside of the submarine enclosure, the money collected for naval charities.

As soon as the war had finished the council had discussed if it would be possible to obtain some **WAR TROPHIES**, in particular guns that could be placed on the sea front for the interest of the following year's visitors. They approached the War Office Trophies Committee, which had been set up by the government to allocate some of the spoils of war to towns and cities across the country. The town was offered a damaged German machine gun, an ammunition box and ammunition belt and a Field gun captured by the 7th Battalion, The Norfolk Regiment. These were accepted, although there was disappointment that they had been offered a damaged gun, and placed on Hall Quay. The town then received a German mine, at first this was kept in the vestibule of the Town Hall but later moved outside onto Hall Quay, near the Post Office. On 5 February a sale of surplus and salvaged military equipment was held at the Barracks and the council purchased a large quantity of barbed wire and other military stores. Another mine, picked up by the drifter *Eveline Joyce* 47 miles east of the town on 8 September 1919, was placed at the foot of the Jetty.

The white ensigns from HMS *Yarmouth* and HMS *Alecto*, together with the Red Cross flag that had flown over the Seafield Hospital and Melton Lodge, were placed in the parish church in 1919. On 19 April, a clock, built by Gillet & Johnson, of Croydon, was fixed to the church tower, celebrating the victory in the Great War. Provided by a local pawnbroker, Mr Fredrick Marsh, at a cost of £350 the clock had a Westminster chime. The church authorities refused to allow the clock to be illuminated. In 1921 the flags from the Air Station and HMS *Roberts* were also placed in the church. On 4 December 1921 a memorial window was dedicated in the church. The window was inserted in the South Chancel at a cost of £1,500. A Roll of Honour with more than 800 names was also placed in the church. The window and the Roll were dedicated by the Archdeacon of Sheffield but both were later to be destroyed when the church was bombed in 1942.

Men were returning from war service in ever increasing numbers and in January 1919 182 Yarmouth men who had been prisoners of war were given a dinner at Goode's Rooms and afterwards entertained at the Regent Theatre. Each man was also given £3. On 1 February 130 Yarmouth men who had been prisoners of war were among 1,050 Norfolk men at a reception at Blackfriars Hall in Norwich. The Mayor of Yarmouth attended this event and the men were entertained with a concert, following the speeches and tea.

The National War Savings Committee offered the town a tank as a war trophy and this was delivered to Beach railway station on 3 December 1919. One of 264 tanks presented to towns and cities across the country this 30-ton tank, named Kiwi, was driven to the Hall Quay under its own power and placed on an ornamental plinth. The engine and other fittings were then removed. The townsfolk could now see with their own eyes for the first time what a real tank looked like. The tank remained near the entrance to the Town Hall for several years until removed and scrapped in 1928 when the Hall Quay was realigned in preparation for the opening of the new Haven Bridge. One offer that was refused by the council was an aeroplane, presumably from the South Denes Air Station that had brought down a Zeppelin.

Throughout 1919 submarines continued to be seen in the port. On 29 March a large German submarine minelayer was brought in, escorted by two British H-class submarines, and moored at Brush Quay. The boat was rusty and in a dilapidated condition, stripped of most of its fittings and had been found abandoned in the North Sea. This caused considerable interest among the townsfolk and large crowds gathered at the quayside to see the submarine.

On 20 June 1919 the Admiral of the Fleet, The Earl Beatty, was given the Freedom of the Borough in a ceremony in the Town Hall.

On 29 March 1919 a German submarine, on the right, was brought into the port by two H-Class British submarines. This caused considerable interest and large crowds gathered on the quay to see the boats.

In July another German submarine, the *Deutschland* , moored at the quay opposite Queen Street. Again, as can be seen from the large crowd, this also caused considerable interest and was a popular post-war attraction.

Beatty had become Commander in Chief of the Grand Fleet in the latter part of the war and in that capacity he received the surrender of the German High Seas Fleet at the end of the war. Earl Beatty arrived from Holkham Hall, where he had been staying, with Lady Beatty and Lord and Lady Leicester.

Soon after the war had finished the Council began to plan the **PEACE CELEBRATIONS** and authorised £2,500 to cover the costs. The celebrations were held on 18 and 19 July 1919. On the first day there was a school children's parade and entertainment and in the evening a dinner was given to the inhabitants of the Borough, discharged, demobilised and serving members on leave of HM Forces and Boy Scouts with war service. To accommodate such a large number of people the dinner was held at eight locations, Goode's Rooms on Marine Parade, York Road Drill Hall, Nelson Road Drill Hall, Savoy Hotel on Regent Road, Hill's Restaurant in King Street, Arcade Restaurant on the Marine Parade, Gorleston Pavilion and the Town Hall. All dinners began at 7.15 p.m. and the mayor and mayoress visited each group during the evening. On Saturday there was a 'Grand Decorated, Historical and Emblematical Car and Trade Cart Procession' followed by a firework display on the beach opposite

The Declaration of Peace being read by the Town Clerk outside the Town Hall on 28 June 1919. The ceremony included sheathing the Sword of Justice, seen on the Clerk's left, which had, by tradition, remained unsheathed since war was declared in 1914.

Trafalgar Square, a bonfire on Gorleston Cliffs and a 'line of fire', beacons stretching from Gorleston Cliffs to Sandown Road.

Under the terms of the armistice Germany had been required to surrender all its submarines to Britain. Many of these visited ports around the country, causing great interest and one such visitor to Great Yarmouth was the *Deutschland,* a large submarine built in 1916. Large crowds turned out to see her as she was towed into port on 31 July 1919 and moored opposite Queen Street. After the war Horatio Bottomley, an outspoken publisher who had established the patriotic magazine John Bull in 1906, had bought this vessel. Throughout the war Bottomly had argued that Germany 'must be wiped of the map of Europe'. The *Deutschland* had been the first of the large German submarines built to beat the British blockade of the North Sea by carrying cargo between America and Germany. The submarine was exhibited on behalf of the King George's Fund for Sailors.

From 14 to 22 September four battleships from the First Battle Squadron visited the town. They were the *Revenge, Resolution, Ramillies* and the *Royal Oak.* The ships anchored off the town and visitors were taken out by boat to be shown around, the crews attending several functions in the town including sporting events.

Until the aftermath of the Great War there were no **WAR MEMORIALS** in the sense we are now familiar with in this country. The government decided it was not practical to repatriate the remains of all the soldiers killed abroad and therefore there would be few domestic graves on which grieving relatives could focus their loss. The only graves were those of men who had been brought back wounded and subsequently died. This led to the erection of war memorials as surrogate headstones for the thousands of men who had died in action. The countries national memorial, the Cenotaph, was erected in Whitehall in London. A cenotaph is a monument erected to a person whose body lies elsewhere. Designed by Sir Edwin Lutyens the stone block has only two inscriptions: 'The Glorious Dead' and 'MCMXIV – MCMXIX'. King George V unveiled it on 11 November 1920, on the second anniversary of the armistice. Thousand of memorials were soon to follow, erected in almost every village, town and city in the country, some large, some small, some in churchyards others on village greens.

The motorcade carrying Admiral Beatty along Regent Street on 20 June 1919 after he had received the Freedom of the Borough.

The war memorial in St George's Park was unveiled by HRH Prince Henry on 7 January 1922 and dedicated by the Bishop of Norwich.

In Great Yarmouth it was decided that the town memorial should be erected in St. George's Park. Rather ambitiously the first design was commissioned from Sir Edwin Lutyens, designer of the Cenotaph, the estimates for building a memorial to his design varying from £7,000 to over £10,000. By the spring of 1921 the town had been unable to raise sufficient money and the project was reluctantly abandoned. A local architect, Mr F.R.B. Haward, then stepped in, offering to design a memorial and take no payment, only out-of-pocket expenses. A list of names to be placed on the memorial was drawn up but it did not, like several other memorials, include civilians. As a result the names of Samuel Smith and Martha Taylor, even though they had been the first ever casualties in the country to perish in an air raid, were not included. The completed memorial was unveiled on 7 January 1922 by His Royal Highness Prince Henry and dedicated by the Bishop of Norwich. A stone memorial was erected in Gorleston cemetery and one of a similar design in the Yarmouth cemetery at Caister. In some places the war memorial took a very different form; in the village of Caister a new organ was installed in the parish church in July 1920 and dedicated as the memorial to the 49 men from the village who lost their lives in the Great War.

Memorials were erected in many schools and work places. These included the Edward Worlledge school where a large wooden memorial, recording the 456 'Old Worlledgers' who had served their country, was unveiled on 23 December 1920. On 1 December 1921 a combined memorial to the Old Boys of three schools was unveiled in the Nelson School (now St George's). The wooden plaque included the names of past pupils from the British School (which stood on the corner of St George's Road and Nelson Road) and the Trafalgar Road School (which later became the Girls High School). This plaque has recently been restored by the Preservation Trust. A memorial plaque was placed in the Grammar School on Salisbury Road (now the High School) while a stone memorial, once in the now demolished Church Road School at Gorleston, is in store. While several other memorials still exist many others have disappeared over the years. Among the work places to install memorial plaques was the Post Office in Regent Street.

THE GREAT WAR – A TIMELINE

A few events have been included (*in italics*) to place the local dates in context with the war in general.

1913

Several visits by submarines from their base at Harwich.

April 15	A Royal Naval Air Station is established on the South Denes with a Headquarters set up at 25 Regent Street.

1914

The Volunteer Training Corps and ladies War Workers Assn. established.

June 28	*Archduke Franz Ferdinand and his wife Duchess Sophie assassinated.*
August 4	*United Kingdom declares war on Germany.*
August 4	*British Expeditionary Force arrives in France.*
August	A submarine base established at Bryant's Quay. HMS *Alecto,* the depot ship, moored at the quay.
August	The Naval Base, HMS *Kingfisher*, is established on the Gorleston side of the river near Baker Street.
August	The Coastguard Station, on Marine Parade, is taken over as accommodation for men at the Air Station.
November 3	The first coastal bombardment by German war ships. No damage or casualties.
November	The Crossley Auxiliary Red Cross hospital established in a building on the South Denes.

1915

An Anti-Aircraft gun is placed on Gorleston Cliffs and another at Caister.

January 19	The first Zeppelin air raid on this country. Yarmouth bombed. Damage to property in St Peter's Plain and on Fishwharf, two people killed.
February 6	The Mayor issues instructions to every household, what to do in case of invasion.
March 20	'Seafield' Red Cross Auxiliary hospital opened.
April 25	*Allied forces land on Gallipoli.*
May 7	*The liner RMS* Lusitania *sunk by German U-Boats. 1,198 people drowned, 761 survived.*
May	An Auxiliary Patrol Base is established at Bollard Quay. The aircraft kept in a hangar on Boundary Road.
July	*National Registration Act.* All residents required to register at the Town Hall. Gorleston Pavilion becomes a Navy & Military Social Club.
December 26	The Cliff Hotel destroyed by fire. Used by the Naval Base as a headquarters.

1916

Pillboxes built either side of Acle Road and on the Breydon wall.
Council declares it is nearly bankrupt.

January	*The Military Services Act brings in conscription.*
March	*A national fund raising event, War Ship week.*
April 25	The second coastal bombardment by German warships. No casualties but minor damage.
April 13	King George V visits the Naval Base and the Air Station.

85

May 31	*Two day battle of Jutland begins.*
May	A Monitor ship, HMS *Roberts*, is moored in the harbour opposite he lifeboat sheds to protect the town.
June	The Corton lightship is blown up. Five killed.
July 1	*First day of the Battle of the Somme. 19,000 British troops died.*
November 28	Zeppelin L21 shot down by Flt Lt Cadbury flying from the Air Station.
November	The town's first War Shrine is unveiled by the mayor in Victoria Street.

1917

April 6	*America enters the war.*
May 10	Cobholm War Shrine unveiled by the mayor.
June 13	*First Gotha heavy bomber raid on London.*

1918

January 14	The third and last bombardment of the town by German war ships. Four people killed. Minor damage to property.
February	*Food rationing introduced.*
March	*The RNAS and the RFC become the RAF.*
March	Melton Lodge replaces Seafield as a Red Cross Auxiliary hospital.
April	Tank Week, a national fund raising event. The town decorates a tram as it is not allocated a real tank. Money raised £183,000.

July 4	American troops (600) visit the town to play Baseball on the Wellesley. Given a reception by Mayor.
August 5	Zeppelin L70 shot down by Major Cadbury. *This is the last air raid on this country.*
Nov 11	*Germany signs the Armistice. Fighting ends at 11 a.m.* The mayor announces the Armistice at 12.30 from the town hall balcony. A parade through the town follows.

1919

January 17	Melton Lodge Red Cross Auxiliary hospital is closed.
April 19	A clock is fixed to Parish Church tower to celebrate victory.
June 20	Admiral Beatty is given the Freedom of the Borough.
July 18-19	Peace Celebrations. Dinners, fireworks and processions in the town.
July 31	A German submarine, *Deutschland,* on view at Hall Quay.
September 9	The Auxiliary Patrol Base at Bollard Quay is closed.
December 3	A tank is placed on Hall Quay. Given to the town by the Government Trophies of War committee. (Removed 1929)

1920

January 10	*The official end of the Great War.*

1921

December 4	A Memorial window unveiled in the parish church.

1922

January 7	The war memorial in St George's Park is unveiled by HRH Prince Henry.

BIBLIOGRAPHY

Books:

Allingham H. *Kitchener's Last Volunteer*, Mainstream, 2008.
Barker T. *Transport in Great Yarmouth,* Vol. I, 1980.
Bird C. *Silent Sentinels*, Lark's Press, 1999.
Castle M. *History of the Great Yarmouth Battery*, Jarrolds, 1927.
Cronin R. *RN Shipboard Aircraft Development*, Air Britain, 1990.
Davies P. *History of Medicine in Great Yarmouth*, Paul Davies, 2003.
Davies P. *The Parish Church of St Nicholas*, Paul Davies, 2007.
Doyle P. *First World War Britain*, Shire, 2012.
Gamble C. Snowden. *The Story of a North Sea Air Station*, Spearman, 1967.
Hawkins L. *The Ocean Fleet of Yarmouth*, Private pub. 1983.
Kent P. *Fortifications of East Anglia*, Terrance Dalton, 1988
Maltster R. *Maritime Norfolk part 2*, Poppyland, 2013.
Meers F. *Norfolk in the First World War*, Phillimore, 2004.
Storey N. *Norfolk in the Great War*, Halsgrove, 2008.
Wyatt R. *Death from the Skies*, Giddion, 1990.

Papers and Journals.

Cross & Cockade Journal Vol. 12 No 1, Vol. 21 No 2, Vol. 35 No 4.
Great Yarmouth Borough Council Minute Books, 1913-1919.
Great Yarmouth Mercury, 1914-1919.
Lewis C. Unpublished notes, 1983, Time & Tide Museum.
Rye G. Great Yarmouth Fortifications, GYAS Journal, 1987.
Yarmouth Independent, 1914-1919.

INDEX

89

PETER ALLARD COLLECTION

One of the town's trams converted to resemble a tank in April 1918, (see also page 44). The tram is seen here in King Street, outside the building housing the Freeman, Hardy & Willis shoe shop. This building was later demolished when the Central Arcade (now the Victoria Arcade) was built in 1926. The stalemate of trench warfare in 1915 led to the development of the tank. At first called 'land ships' they were given the name tank to preserve secrecy and because they resembled steel water tanks. The first use of tanks on the battlefield was in September 1916.